"Here is your country. Cherish these natural wonders, cherish the natural resources, cherish the history and romance as a sacred heritage, for your children and your children's children. Do not let selfish men or greedy interests skin your country of its beauty, its riches or its romance."

~ Theodore Roosevelt~

Sahara's Plight

Nature's Guardians Series Book 3

Written and Illustrated

by
Alisha M. Risen-Kent

Sahara's Plight is a work of fiction. Any resemblance (excepting the Conservation page) of characters, names, places, or incidents to reality is pure coincidence.

For more information, you can contact me at
skydancer792007@yahoo.com or at the Nature's Guardians
website www.naturesguardiansbookseries.com

Dedication

For my children, who are my strength and motivation, my whole world.

For my parents, who always believed in my dream. Mom, thanks for always pushing me to never give up and being there for me through all the ups and downs life throws my way.

For my beta and best friend, without whom I would have never found the courage to write this.

Lastly, to all my family and friends who encouraged me along the way.

Acknowledgements

I would like to give a special shout out to all those who helped me write this book.

Thanks, Vasco Galante at Gorongosa National Park. Your information about the park, its past and its present, was essential for the story.

Thanks to the wonderful people at the Cheetah Conservation Fund. You provided me with great material on cheetah behavior.

Lastly, thank-you to the Fossil Rim Wildlife Center for the information on cheetah behavior in captivity.

Translations:

Swahili:

Asha: life

French:

ma petite: my little one
oui: yes
non: no
Je suis désolé: I am so sorry!
chaton: kitten
Au revoir: until we meet again
bien: okay

Definitions:

ensconced: settle in a safe place.
skepticism: doubt
impotently: helplessly
coalesced: come together
introverted: keeping to oneself
circumnavigate: go around
chagrined: embarrass
ousted: drive out of a position or place
haphazard: without order
euthanize: put an animal to death

Table of Contents:

Chapter One: Spring

The first thing you notice about Africa in spring is all the green, for as far as the eye can see. Tiny wildflowers dot an ocean of swaying green grasses like stars in the night sky. The bellowing of water buffalo and wildebeest mingle with the braying of zebra in a song to the season. Morning dew glistens like diamonds on flower petals and blades of grass. The dawn is filled with puffs of clouds snorted from the grazers, even as the sun struggles to rise from the darkness.

It is this world I was born into, me and my four siblings. I felt the tremble of the earth before I could either see or hear. The great beasts shook the earth as they moved across the plains. I slept, comforted by my mother's warm body and those of my siblings. Before long, my eyes opened onto a world I would soon be part of.

My mother chose her den well. We were ensconced in the hollow of a hill, probably an abandoned burrow of some other creature. From the top of the hill, she had a great vantage point, able to see far into the vast grassland that surrounded us. This afforded her the ability to spot prey that would otherwise be hidden.

Although she raised us alone, she provided for our every need and I can't remember ever going hungry in those early days. By the time my siblings and I were a few weeks old, we had fallen into a routine: wake, nurse, play, and sleep. My brother, N'dugu, however, always tried to be different. From the beginning, his adventurous nature got him into trouble. I lost count of how many times Mother scolded him for trying to follow her out of the burrow.

When we were just a few months old, N'dugu's adventures became ours. We abandoned our safe burrow and followed Mother into the deep grass. As little as we were, we could not see above our hiding place and the noises that reached us left me wondering what creature made the sounds. My mother's presence was a comfort to me. I knew she would protect us. The further we ventured from our burrow, however, the more we traveled into the unknown. Little did we know of all the dangers we would face in the weeks to come and not all of us would make it through.

"N'dugu!" I cried for the hundredth time. "You know Mother said not to leave the brush."

My oldest brother sighed and turned to me. "Geez, Sahara. I'm just takin' a peek. Nothing will happen and if you don't say anything, Mother will never know."

"You can't keep disobeying her," I said, walking over to him. "You put us all in danger."

"Have you even seen these 'monsters' Mother speaks of?" he asked. "She only says that so we will do what she says."

"I don't have to see them. I can hear them."

N'dugu wouldn't listen. He never did. So, against our mother's wishes, he made his way to the edge of our hiding place. Before he could catch a glimpse of what lay beyond, Mother poked her head inside, her eyes narrowed. She glared down at him from her impressive height. In response, N'dugu smiled as only a cheetah could, flashing his needle-sharp baby teeth in mock innocence.

"Hello, Mother," he said, sitting on his haunches. His wild baby hair fluffed out around him, making for a comical picture. "I was just coming to greet you. How was the hunt?"

Mother closed her eyes and sighed. "N'dugu, one of these days..."

Mother said this every time N'dugu did something to disappoint her. We always wondered what came after that phrase but she never finished it. Instead, she lifted him up by his scruff and carried him back to where the rest of us rested. I could see the indignation on his face and tried hard not to laugh. It was the least he deserved.

Mother laid down with N'dugu still in her jaws. He struggled to get away as soon as she released some of the pressure but she pulled him back with a massive paw. To his ultimate horror, she began to clean him, her rough tongue smoothing the tawny fur of his back.

"Mom, this is embarrassing!" he cried. "I can do it myself."

Mother just ignored him and continued with her cleaning. Resigned, N'dugu flipped over onto his back and sighed. Mother, oblivious to his dramatic act, began cleaning the spotted fur of his belly. I couldn't hold back my laughter any longer. My chuckles emboldened my other siblings and they followed my lead.

Without missing a beat or even looking our way, Mother said, "I don't know why you're laughing. You're next."

N'dugu smirked as our laughter stopped and we ran to find hiding places. Well, most of us ran. My youngest sibling and only sister, Nahi, looked forward to alone time with Mother and waited patiently for her to finish with N'dugu. Nahi was the smallest of us, only half as big as N'dugu, who was the largest. She was also quiet and shy, preferring solitude to group activities. N'dugu, surprisingly, was very protective of her and helped her when she fell behind. His tenderness for our youngest sibling surprised me.

Mother gave N'dugu a final swipe of her tongue and released him. He shook his body and ran off, rolling in the dirt near Nahi. Mother beckoned Nahi closer and the little cub went willingly into Mother's arms.

For the next few weeks, we traveled through the tall grasses, mother leaving occasionally to find food. We fell into a new routine and life was once again comfortable. It was during this time that I noticed something strange about N'dugu. Not only was he more adventurous than the rest of us, his appearance was changing as well. Mother had pebble-sized spots all over her body with smaller ones on her head and legs. This, she told us, was to allow her to blend in with the tall grasses. Me and my siblings all shared this trait, discounting the mane of tawny fur down our backs.

N'dugu, however, had splotches instead of spots and his tail had broad bands around it verses the spots on ours. Most interesting were the three stripes that ran down his back from his head to his tail. While his baby mane had hidden this, it was beginning to show the older he grew. Curious, I approached Mother one night while everyone else slept.

"Sahara, we are moving again tomorrow," she scolded lightly. "You should be sleeping."

"Mother, why does N'dugu look different than the rest of us?"

Mother looked at me closely, as though she were looking for something only she could see. After a quick glance at my sleeping siblings, she beckoned me closer. I curled up next to her and she began her explanation.

"Sahara, when you are a bit older and can see the world as I do, you will notice that our kind are disappearing from the land. There are too many predators and not enough room. The lions and hyena are claiming the most fertile lands for themselves, away from the two-legs, which leaves us much too close to them. The two-legs fear us and believe that we hunt their animals. Because of this, they hunt us. Now, there are too few of us left."

She paused for a moment to gather her thoughts and continued. "Some believe there is a savior coming, a cheetah who will lead us to a better place where we are not hunted and can live in peace. This 'king' will stand out from the rest of us. He will be courageous, strong, and wise. With his guidance, we will once again have our place on the plains.

"Even the two-legs have their legends concerning this king. They call him *nsuifisi*– hyena-leopard, because of the unusual markings on his fur. They fear him because they do not know what his arrival means. It is possible that your brother is this king cheetah."

I thought about what she said but could not imagine N'dugu as anything other than my disobedient and adventurous brother. Needing to speak my thoughts, I looked up at Mother.

"Do you really think N'dugu is wise," I asked.

The look on my face must have shown my skepticism because Mother simply chuckled. She gave me an affectionate nudge before answering my question.

"I think N'dugu has a lot of growing up to do. Perhaps one day he will surprise us all. Now, run along and get some sleep."

Shaking my head in disbelief, I did as she bid and returned to my siblings, curling up among them. With my mind filled with fantastical visions, I drifted off to sleep.

Chapter Two: The Beginning of a Journey

The following weeks were both exciting and scary. My siblings and I continued to grow as we traversed the plains. The green grasses that dominated the land after our birth were beginning to turn yellow as the rains stopped and the land dried out. Sometimes in the night we could hear the roar of far off lions. This frightened us and we crowded closer to Mother. Her warmth reassured us and we slept soundly, comforted by the thought that everything was as it should be.

One morning, we woke to a fog so heavy, we could barely see our noses in front of us. Mother forged a path somewhere in front us, her trail through the grass the only evidence that we still followed her. We could hear something moving not far away, or rather, several somethings. Their heavy footfalls and snorts echoed off the dense clouds.

Mother stopped at one point to allow us to gather around her. Five sets of eyes looked up at her as she scanned around impotently. We could feel the tension rolling off her shoulders.

"Stay close," she whispered. "The herd is nearby and if they sense us, they will charge."

Her worry sobered even N'dugu, who clung to Mother like the rest of us. She led us silently past the grazing herd and into the relative safety of the brush. We watched as she scanned the area again.

"Mother?" I asked when none of my other siblings spoke.

"It's alright, Sahara," she said, turning to look at me. "We'll wait until the fog lifts before we move again."

Her gentle smile reassured me and I leaned against her. From the corner of my eye, I noticed N'dugu sitting slightly off by himself. Lifting my head, I turned to him. He sat straight with his eyes focused on something ahead of him that only he could see. Glancing back to Mother, I noticed a similar look on her face. Perhaps she was right about him.

The fog cleared a short time later. It never lasted long in the summer heat. From our vantage point we could see far into the plains. Sometimes I wondered if Mother had an invisible map in her head. Without realizing it, we had ascended a hill in our trek through the fog. Now that the clouds had lifted, we could see our world as never before. As one, we stared in amazement.

Directly in front of us, near the path we had forged through the grass, were hundreds of wildebeests. They snorted and shook their heads, some grazing and some keeping a watchful eye on the surroundings. Several calves frolicked among the herd, secure amidst the adults.

Off to our right, and scattered among the wildebeests were zebra. They nickered and danced among themselves, their tufted tails beating uselessly at the flies on their flanks. I was mesmerized watching them as one zebra all but disappeared when it moved beside another. They, too, had young, many of which lay resting in the grass.

Toward our left, the grazers thinned out, probably because the brush grew thicker there. A few giraffe meandered among the trees, their long tongues pulling at leaves too high for most grazers to reach. Although they were some distance away, I could sense their great height and I sat in awe of them.

Next to me, Mother shifted. I glanced at her, taking note of where she was looking. I followed her gaze. Far off into the distance, as though they knew we rested there, were impala. I could just barely make out their forms from our shelter. Mother stood suddenly, overbalancing me and I shuffled to my feet.

"Stay here and keep hidden," she said. "It is dangerous out in the open."

We all nodded except for N'dugu, who still sat with his back rigid and eyes focused straight ahead.

"N'dugu," Mother called. "I need you to keep an eye out for your siblings. It will be your responsibility to ensure their safety. Can I count on you?"

N'dugu turned to her, determination on his face. "Yes, Mother."

She nodded and slipped out from under the brush. With one last look at us, she turned and loped off. Five pairs of eyes watched as she disappeared into the grass.

Mother returned that evening with enough food to feed us all. Bellies full, we snuggled up together, taking a few moments to nurse and reaffirm our bonds. Afterwards, we settled down to sleep. Mother had moved away a little since my siblings and I took up so much room. I vaguely noticed her peering into the night, a look of contentment settling over her. Just as I closed my eyes, I felt a nudge from my side.

My overindulging left me sated and tired and the last thing I wanted to do was stay awake. Still, I lifted my head to see which of my siblings wanted my attention. To my surprise, N'dugu peered up at me, his paw against my side. His eyes were bright without a hit of tiredness. I cocked my head to the side, curious to what he wanted. He simply stared at me. Sighing, I shifted until I lay directly in front of him.

"What is it, brother?" I asked trying to mask my irritability.

N'dugu looked away briefly. I could sense something was bothering him but, for some reason, he was having trouble putting it into words.

"N'dugu," I tried again, keeping my voice low so I didn't alert Mother. "Are you alright?"

"I feel strange," he admitted. "When Mother left today, I felt weird."

"How do you mean?"

"Well, for one, I didn't want to wander off like I normally do. Something about what Mother said made me not want to leave. And...I look different than the rest of you. Why is that? Why am I different?"

"Because you are special."

"I don't want to be special," he cried, laying his chin on his paws. "I want to be like everyone else. I know they don't say it, but the others feel differently towards me."

"N'dugu, you are imagining things. Soji, Kana, and Nahi love you as much they love each other. And Mother thinks you are destined for greatness. Besides, you're my favorite brother. Doesn't that count for something?"

"You're so full of yourself!" he laughed. "I am the great N'dugu. Who wouldn't love me?"

"Now who's full of themselves?" I moved next to him and pushed him onto his side with my shoulder. With a flop, I laid against his side using his fluffy mantle as a headrest. "Well, at least you make a good pillow."

I could feel his chuckle through my cheek.

"Thanks, Sahara," he rumbled. "For what it's worth, you're my favorite sister."

We fell asleep soon after with the distant roar of lions as our lullaby.

Chapter Three: Loss

The next few weeks passed the same as the last. We traveled through Mother's territory mostly unmolested. As the summer progressed, however, Mother brought less food to us, either because she was unable to catch it or unable to keep it. We were growing quickly and our need for meat greater. I noticed the tension in Mother's shoulders when she returned empty-handed.

Near the end of summer, our real lessons began. We had been following Mother on her hunts, pulling back only during the chase. On this particular day, we watched as Mother brought down a young impala. The fawn was born late in the season and Mother happened upon it by sheer luck. Instead of killing it, she brought it back to us.

At this point, we were all leg and fluff and had yet to master the running skills needed to hunt on our own. By bringing the fawn to us, it gave us a chance to learn the skills we would need. N'dugu took to the hunt with a flourish. Soji and Kana quickly followed. I sat back to watch the fawn, trying to conserve my energy while looking for a weakness. Nahi, to my surprise, turned away from our brother's prey, as though she were disturbed by it. In fact, she approached Mother and began to suckle. Mother allowed it with patient resignation.

As I turned back around, the exhausted fawn stumbled. I took my chance and darted out after it, catching it unawares. With a swift bite to its throat, I ended its suffering. Nahi stayed with Mother instead of joining us. I brushed off my unease and fed alongside my brothers.

Later that night, after my other siblings were ensconced in the world of dreams, I approached Mother. She turned disapproving eyes to me, like she did every time I approached her after bedtime. The fur of my thinning mantle rose at her look but I continued anyway.

"Mother," I began. "Why did Nahi not join us today?"

"Nahi is not yet ready to be a hunter," she answered.

"But...we are hunters. Won't she fall behind if she doesn't hunt?"

"Sahara, everyone matures differently. Nahi is still quite small and insecure. It will take her longer to master the skills you and your brothers are learning now. You needn't worry. When the time is right, Nahi will hunt as she needs. Does this ease your mind?"

"Yes, Mother."

"You did well today," she said, a knowing gleam in her eyes. "You will be a great hunter one day."

I sat up straighter and puffed out my chest like N'dugu often did. "Thank-you. I did not want the fawn to suffer."

"That is good. As hunters, it is easy to forget the suffering of our prey, especially in times of extreme hunger. By respecting their sacrifice, we separate ourselves from the thoughtless two-legs that hunt animals for sport. Now, go rest."

I left her and curled up between N'dugu and Nahi. Somehow sensing my presence, N'dugu draped his long legs over me and began purring. I chuckled and snuggled closer to him.

Near the end of summer, the plains changed once again. The great herds began to move as one, leaving the once vibrant plains empty and quiet. Mother, who relied heavily on the antelope, had no choice but to follow.

Some weeks into the great migration, we came to a massive river. The herds stomped and snorted along the water's edge but refused to cross. Even Mother, who had hidden us well away from the lumbering beasts, eyed the water with apprehension. We did not cross water unless absolutely necessary so it really did not surprise me. However, our prey did often to escape our pursuit. With a cub-like curiosity, I approached Mother.

"I do not understand," I said, sitting next to her. "Why do they linger at the water's edge?"

She did not look away from the water as she answered my question. "They are afraid of what lives beneath."

"What is that?"

"Crocodiles. Great predators with jaws full of teeth and strong enough to pull even the mighty buffalo down to a watery death. If you watch very closely, you can see them slithering through the water with just their eyes and nose visible. The grazers know they are there but they cannot see them."

I narrowed my eyes and squinted against the light reflected off the water's surface. After a few minutes, I could see what Mother was talking about. There were so many of them! A chill ran down my spine.

"Mother," I whispered, as though the reptiles could hear me. "How are *we* going to cross?"

"Half a day's journey down river is a narrow passage. When the crocodiles begin to feed here, we will head down there and cross. With any luck, all the predators will be here feeding and we can cross unmolested."

"I'm scared."

Mother turned sympathetic eyes to me. "There are a great many things to fear in this world. Even lions fear sometimes. Fear makes you stronger, and wiser."

"Yes, Mother."

She turned back to the huffing herds. Not long after, the first wildebeest launched into the water. It was followed by hundreds more. Mother watched patiently. As the first grazer reached the other side, chaos erupted from the water. The crocodiles had begun their feast.

"It's time to go," Mother said, turning from the slaughter.

As one, we turned and headed downstream, the echoes of dying grazers filling the air. The sound would haunt my dreams for weeks to come.

As the sun began its descent, we found the place where the river narrowed. It was still a great swath of water and I was apprehensive of crossing it. However, all was quiet. We scanned the water and banks for any sign of crocodiles. Mother, confident all the predators were away, stepped into the warm water.

"The current is strong here," she said, looking back. "Stay close and keep up."

N'dugu followed right behind her and I was right behind him. I noticed belatedly that Nahi hung back. She hesitated entering the water. The current was too strong for me to turn back for her so I continued to follow N'dugu. We were half-way across the river before she joined us. I wanted to warn Mother but anytime I opened my mouth, water rushed in. As soon as my feet touched the other side, I twisted around to find her.

"Mother, Nahi!" I called

"I know." She, too, had turned to find her youngest cub.

Nahi struggled against the current. N'dugu ran past me to aid her but Mother stopped him.

"I must help her!" he cried.

"You cannot." The sorrow in Mother's voice had my head spinning back to our tiny sister.

Cutting through the current was a long reptilian tail heading straight for Nahi. We all called for her to hurry but we knew the crocodile would reach her before she reached safety. Just passed mid-river, she disappeared, pulled beneath the mirky waters. She never resurfaced. We cried for our lost sibling as Mother turned us from her watery grave.

"Why did you not let me save her?" N'dugu growled at Mother.

"Because then, I would have lost both of you." Her sorrow-filled eyes quieted N'dugu. "We must find what is left of the herds and rest."

We did not speak the rest of the way. N'dugu, perhaps sensing my troubled heart, leaned against me as we walked. His closeness was a balm to my pain. Once we found the herds, we curled tightly around each other and Mother, who usually slept away from us, wrapped herself around us. Sleep did not come easily with our minds full of death and sorrow.

Chapter Four: On Our Own

By the end of the next summer, a full turn of the seasons later, my siblings and I were as big as Mother. We had all but mastered the hunt and followed along when Mother brought down prey. It took all of us working together to ensure we had enough to eat, especially in N'dugu's case. He towered over the rest of us. While we still sported a bit of baby fluff along our backs, most of our coats were as elegant as Mother's. N'dugu stood out more than ever. His coat was regal and exquisite and longer than ours. I often rubbed against him just to feel the silkiness. Of course, this irritated him and he would push me in a half-hearted attempt to keep me away.

Mother, perhaps sensing our growing need for independence, would venture off alone, sometimes for days on end, leaving us to our own devices. For the most part, we managed well without her. I knew a change was coming and that soon, we would be on our own for good. When she left, N'dugu would fill her place, directing hunts and resting sites. We followed him naturally, as though he were made for the job. I began to see what Mother had talked about so long ago. My brother was a natural leader.

When the rains came again, we knew our time with Mother was at an end. Our games of play had become feats of survival and Mother watched it from afar. One evening, as we all gathered in what protection we could, Mother approached us. She had been distant for so long that her presence surprised us. She laid down and faced the four of us.

"I am so very proud of all of you," she said. "You have grown up to be amazing hunters and I know you will rule the plains for a long time to come. Our time is at an end. Now, you must forge your own paths in the world. I have but a few more pieces of wisdom to share with you. Your life is more important than your prey. Do not fight other predators for it. It is better to let them have it and live another day. We are not built for fighting. Keep away from other predators. There is not enough room left for everyone and if you run into something bigger than yourself, you will lose. Lastly, stay away from the two-legs. They are dangerous, even if they do not seem to be. They will take your life easier than anything else on the plains."

We stared at her wide-eyed. I did not want to say good-bye to my mother but I knew she was right. It was time to face the world without her. She stood and butted her head against each of ours, her form of affection. We mewled at the contact. When she reached N'dugu, she stopped.

"Watch over your siblings," she said. "They will need you in the coming months. Be strong and courageous and wise. I suspect we will all need you in the future."

N'dugu puffed out his impressive chest and nodded. "I will, Mother. Someday, I will save us all."

Mother chuckled and butted his head. Without another word, she turned and loped away.

We stayed together after Mother left, content to hunt and sleep side by side. I think having us all together helped ease the loss of our mother. We had each other and as long as we had that, everything seemed right with the world. The rains came and went, leaving the plains once again splendid and green. The lakes and rivers overflowed their banks and the cool dew covered everything. With such abundance, the grazers timed their births to give their young the greatest chance at survival. We fed well during that time and most other predators let us be.

Toward the beginning of summer, just as the grasses started to yellow, we spotted our first two-legs. They came in something as big as a buffalo that made a noise we'd never heard before. Although it seemed to have feet, it moved across the plains like a snake, never lifting them. The two-legs were inside the beast, as though the thing had eaten them. We were some ways off when they stopped. N'dugu sat up and watched them with apprehension but they did not come closer. After some time, they moved on, leaving us in peace once again.

"We must go deeper into the plains," N'dugu said.

"But the lions are there," I cried. "And the migration is about to start."

"We do not have a choice, Sahara." He turned worried eyes to me. "You know what Mother said. The two-legs are worse than any other predator on the plains. They know we are here and I'm certain they will be back."

I whimpered, realizing he was right. Soji and Kana nodded their heads in understanding. As one, we got to our feet and made our way deeper into the plains. Surprisingly, the herds grew thicker the deeper we traveled and for a moment, I thought everything would be fine. With this much prey, surely we would be just fine, especially if we all stuck together.

That night, however, the hair along my spine stood up at the array of new sounds bombarding my ears. The cackles of hyena filled the air far too close to where we rested and not far off was the roar of a lion. N'dugu, sensing my unease, moved closer to me. Even Soji and Kana moved closer, either for my comfort or their own. It was a long night and I woke feeling less than rested.

The next morning, we cautiously scanned the area for viable prey. Buffalo and wildebeest were really too big and strong for us to take down so we concentrated our hunting on impala. Unfortunately, there were none in this part of the plains. N'dugu sat deep in thought as our stomachs growled impatiently. Soji, unable to endure the silence, approached N'dugu.

"What are you thinking, brother?" he asked.

"If we work together, we may be able to bring down that wildebeest," he answered, nodding to an old male with a slight limp.

"I suppose, if the others don't turn to his aid."

"Kana," N'dugu called. Our youngest brother loped up to him. "Do you think we can do it?"

"Sure. If one of us scatters the herd, the old one may trip and the rest of us can take him down. It would be enough to feed all of us."

"Good. Sahara, you are our best runner. I will leave the herd to you but keep your distance. If one of them kicks you, it will be bad."

"Understood." I wasn't looking forward to burning precious energy on a "maybe" but my stomach would give me no end of grief until I fed it.

Circling around the heard, I waited until my brothers were in position before springing out of the brush. As expected, the herd scattered. I chased them without rhyme or reason, allowing my brothers to bring down our prey. Once I was sure the herd wouldn't turn back, I went to join N'dugu and the others. I flopped down next to them, thoroughly exhausted. They were nearly finished when I gathered enough strength to eat my fill. It was a good hunt and we slept with full bellies that night.

Chapter Five: Survival

Despite moving further into the plains, the two-legs' pursuit do not stop. Sometimes, we only heard their moving contraption. Worse, the deeper we traveled, the closer we moved to the other predators. As it was, one of us always stayed awake at night on the lookout for danger. The lions were closer. I could nearly feel their breath on the back of my neck. Concerned, I confronted N'dugu.

"Brother, I know the two-legs are dangerous but how far do you intend to travel to avoid them?" I asked a few weeks after entering the lions' territory.

"As far as we have to. I will not risk them getting too close." N'dugu searched the plains for antelope but we had seen precious little since moving this far in.

"I understand, but we must follow the herds. Already they are moving on. If we don't keep up with them, we will starve."

N'dugu sighed and closed his eyes. "I know, sister. I just wish the two-legs would move on."

"Maybe they aren't even here for us," I said, a sudden thought filling my mind. "Maybe they are here for the lions. If we slip away in the night and catch up with the herds, maybe the two-legs will lose our trail."

He turned to me and stared as though I were a stranger. "I hadn't thought of that. You're brilliant! Go find Soji and Kana. Tell them to rest up and we will leave as soon as it is dark."

I nodded and left to find my brothers. If we could find the herds, we'd find the impala. I was looking forward to going to bed with a full belly. I found Soji and Kana shortly after and told them of the plan. They agreed it was the best one and, after finding shelter from the blazing summer sun, we settled down to wait out the day.

A week after leaving the lions' territory, we located the herds. The impala were fat and sated in their summer grounds, the fawns big enough to provide a hearty meal. Surprisingly, there didn't seem to be many other predators. Nights were quiet and daytime hunts went smoothly. Most of the large prey had already crossed the river of death, as we called it, leaving the smaller prey too scared to face the waters. I knew we needed to cross eventually but I was in no hurry to relive the past. Nor were my brothers. Nahi's loss was still fresh in our memories, despite the two years that had passed.

As predicted, the two-legs did not follow, either because they could not find us, or they were indeed there for the lions. Mother once said the strange creatures had a fascination with the large predators. I could not understand the appeal. To me, lions weren't that attractive. They had dull coats with no patterns, heavy bodies, and loose jaws. And the males were lazy, requiring females to hunt for them. Who would be fascinated by that? Well, I never pretended to understand the two-legs.

We settled along the river for the next few weeks. By the end of summer, our prey had become wise, realizing there was a threat on land as great as what lie in the river. When the last herds of wildebeest, buffalo, and zebra made to cross the river, the impala followed suit, hoping to hide within their numbers. We had no choice but to follow.

N'dugu led us downriver, as our mother had done. Once we reached the spot we would cross, we hesitated. It was silly, really. Back then, we were

cubs. Now, we were full grown and strong with full
bellies. The chances of a crocodile getting us now
were unlikely. Still, our memories haunted us.

"It's now or never," N'dugu said. "We will go in as
one. Make as little sound as possible." He turned to
see our frightened eyes. "We can do this. Listen."

We did. The herds upstream made a terrible
racket. The crocodiles wouldn't even hear us enter
the water. Moving side by side, we stepped in
together. The crossing was uneventful and we
reached the other side without so much as a bump
underwater. The herds were already making their
way into the grasses on the other side. With the
sound of the dying behind us, we ran to catch up with
them.

The rest of the summer passed and the grasses
withered and died. Watering holes dried up and
predators and prey alike fought for what was left. It
was a bounty for my brothers and I. Prey, too weak
to flee became our nourishment. However, with

water becoming scarce, we were forced to share what we had with other predators, like lions and hyena. It was a waiting game that we were determined to win.

Just before the rains returned, when we were too exhausted to chase down anything, we once again heard the two-legs. Somehow, they had followed the herds' migration route and found us. The plains were scorched bare and the heat from the sun was unbearable during the day. What the two-legs found so fascinating, I would never understand. But this time, they did not observe and leave peacefully.

N'dugu, Soji, Kana, and I were resting beneath a leafless tree, the gnarled branches so entangled it provided enough shade to keep us from overheating. From far off, we heard the two-legs' contraption. Heat simmered off the ground so we could not make out the shape but we knew that something was coming. Around us lived nothing but dried out earth. If we ran, assuming we could even gather enough strength to get to our feet, we would be out in the open and vulnerable. Our only chance was to lie low and hope they passed by without seeing us.

It seemed to take forever for the two-legs to reach us. Sound traveled forever on the baked plains and the heat made one see things that weren't there. So long did the noise vibrate the earth, we began to think we were imagining the whole thing. I was unsure if the contraption was simply moving slowly or if it was there at all. After some time, I'd decided that it was just a trick of the heat, that the two-legs had not found us and we were safe.

As the contraption moved closer, however, we knew it was fruitless to hope for that. N'dugu turned to me, tension radiating off his frame.

"I will distract them while you three run," he said.

"No, N'dugu," I said, getting to my feet. "They need you. All of our kind needs you. I will do this."

"Sahara-"

"You know it's true. Do what you were destined to do, brother."

Before he could stop me, I loped out of our cover and toward the two-legs. I didn't dare look back to see if they'd fled. Through the haze, I watched as several two-legs stepped from the contraption holding odd looking sticks out in front of them, as though to ward me off. I had no intention of getting that close. I did, however, examine them. My mind could not wrap itself around these odd creatures. How they managed to stay standing baffled me. Equally baffling was what they had draped over their frames. It seemed like it would be encumbering in a hunt.

I hesitated in my approach. Unlike other predators, I did not feel ill will from these creatures. They did not look on me as a threatening predator would. In fact, even their sticks were resting against their chest and not out in a defensive posture. I flicked my tail in curioslty. Perhaps they were just as curious as I. Then, the words of my mother came back to me.

"Do not trust the two-legs. They are deceitful and pretend to be harmless. That is when they will kill you."

With that memory playing in my mind, I resumed my approach. Before I made it half-way, I felt a sharp sting in my hip. I stumbled and fell, rolling across the dusty earth. I chanced a glance behind me to see my brothers in a similar situation. As I struggled to find my feet, a heavy fog filled my head.

"Shh," said one of the two-legs as they approached me. "It will be all right. We're taking you somewhere safe."

I could not make sense of the words. What was this creature saying? Where were my brothers. I tried to move my head, anything, but my body would not respond. I had a strange feeling of floating over the ground as they picked me up and put me in their contraption. The sun bore down on me and I thought I was going to die right then. I felt a sudden shift and registered N'dugu's face just inches from mine. A few minutes later, my other brothers followed. The two-legs climbed in with us and took us from the only home we'd ever known.

Chapter Six: A New Home

I don't remember much of the trip, except for the rumbling of the surface beneath me. It lulled me into a dazed-like stupor where dreams and reality coalesced. When I finally broke free of the haze, I opened my eyes to find myself trapped. All around me were tree branches, or at least I thought they were branches. With my head still fuzzy, I stumbled to my feet. The motion of the vehicle beneath me did not help but I eventually got my feet under me. A sudden jolt had me slamming against the branches. I whimpered in pain at the contact. They were hard as stone! I tested my teeth on them just to be sure.

Unable to escape, I took in my tiny surroundings. Something was covering my prison but I could tell night had fallen. If not for my superior vision, I would have been blinded. The rattling of the vehicle and my prison echoed loudly in my ears and, try as I might, I could not locate my brothers by sound alone. I squeaked out a weak call, hoping they could hear me over the noise. When no response came, I tried again.

Finally, on my third attempt, N'dugu answered back. He sounded as weak as me but I was grateful he was still with me. Shortly after, Soji and Kana answered as well. At least we were still all together. I huddled down on my belly. My head still felt fuzzy and I wanted all my strength when the two-legs opened my prison.

Some time later, I woke to the heat of the blazing sun baring down on my prison. Even with the covering, I was sweltering. I desperately needed water. As if the two-legs could sense my distress, the conveyance stopped. What did I know? Perhaps they could see into my head. The edge of the cover lifted to reveal a pale, hairless face. I snarled and jumped back. When it became apparent the creature intended to stay, I took a moment to really look at it. A shaggy mane sat atop its head, like that of a lion and was as golden as the sun. Eyes, positioned too close together, simmered blue as the sky.

It opened its mouth and flashed blunted white teeth at me, exposing inadequate canines. I couldn't understand how this creature survived in the world. Was it predator or prey? My golden eyes flashed in warning as it shifted to the side. Another two-legs approach my prison carrying a vessel overflowing with life-giving water. This one was dark everywhere the first one was light. It's skin was the color of rich soil with a short mane of jet black. Even its eyes were dark as the night. It carefully slid the water through an opening in my prison and backed away.

The pale two-legs continued to watch me. I did not want to move closer to it, despite my ravenous thirst. The clear water called to me and my throat burned with need. *Why does it continue to stare?* I thought. *If only it would move I could quench my thirst.*

"It will be alright, *ma petite*," the creature said with a deep voice, as though I could understand it. "Soon, you will be able to make a new life for yourself safe from danger."

With one last lingering look, it backed away and dropped the cover. I pounced on the vessel holding the water, the liquid splashing over the side in my haste. For the first time, I noticed something around my neck. It was slightly restricting and cumbersome. Shaking my head, I realized I could not dislodge it. Too thirsty to really care, I dismissed it as a problem for another day.

Once my belly was full and my thirst sated, I sat back on my haunches. With the vehicle stopped, I could make out the other sounds around me, including those of my brothers. Soji and Kana were drinking their water but N'dugu seemed preoccupied. I suspected the two-legs moved their fascination from me to him.

A loud clash rocked the vehicle and I knew N'dugu had slammed against his prison. His hissing penetrated the air around me. The two-legs scuffled in the dirt, probably escaping my brother's ire. I would, too, if I were them. If anyone could break through the stone branches around us, it was N'dugu. A fluttering reached my ears, which meant the two-legs had dropped his cover and backed away.

"N'dugu," I chirped. "Are you alright?"

"Yes," he answered. "We need to get away from these creatures but I can't break through the branches."

"I know. I tried as well and nearly broke a tooth. What do you think they are going to do to us?"

"I don't know. Get some rest. As soon as they remove the branches, we need to run past them. It's our only chance."

I laid down and rested my head on my paws. The water sat heavy in my belly and combined with the heat, it made me drowsy. Unable to fight it, I closed my eyes and drifted off to sleep.

We stayed in our prisons for two more days and nights. The two-legs continued to give us water and even small bits of meat, some fowl I'd never eaten before. By the time we reached wherever it was we were going, we were well feed and well rested. The sun had been up only a short time when the vehicle stopped. The two-legs jumped to the ground and walked around to where we were. With a flourish they removed the covers from all of our prisons. N'dugu and Soji looked well but Kana stay resting on his belly. I was worried about his lack of energy.

"Kana," I chirped. "Get up! We need to run as soon as they let us out."

"I can't," he cried. "Something is wrong with my stomach. It hurts!"

"N'dugu!" I turned to my oldest brother with worried eyes. He moved toward Kana's prison.

"Just a little longer, brother," he said soothingly. "Once we are free, we can rest all you want."

With a whimper, he pulled his feet under him and stood. The two-legs seemed oblivious to our conversation, lost in their own off to the side. As one, they turned and approached the vehicle. It took two of them to lift our prisons and set them on the ground some distance away from the vehicle. Once all four were on the ground, they stood back.

With them out of the way, I took in the new surroundings. I had to admit that it was beautiful. Despite the harsh summer, these plains were still lush and green. I could smell water nearby and hear the large grazers some distance away. Was this going to be our new home? I turned to N'dugu to see a similar question in his eyes.

After a few minutes, the two-legs approached us again. All together, they lifted the front part of our prisons, allowing us to run free. N'dugu and Soji did not hesitate. They disappeared into the long grass before I'd barely cleared the stone branches of my prison. I turned to find Kana. He was struggling to find his feet. Turning worried eyes on the two-legs, I noticed them watching Kana with concern. If he didn't move soon, they would never let him go.

"Come on, Kana!" I yelled. "I will help you but we have to get away from the two-legs."

I ran up to him as he left his prison and pushed against his shoulder. The move seemed to give him energy and we loped off together. Once we were safely in the security of the grass, I turned again to face the two-legs. They flashed their teeth at one another and clapped each other on the back. Flashing teeth must have been a sign of friendship for them. In every other creature, it is a hostile sign. Two-legs were such strange creatures!

Kana nudged me and I turned, following him through the grass to where N'dugu and Soji waited. Together we traversed our new home. We found shelter soon after, a shallow burrow, and decided to rest the remainder of the day. Kana collapsed, grateful for the respite. He curled around himself, still complaining of pain in his stomach. I worried about my youngest brother. It was dangerous to be so vulnerable. We laid next to him, giving him what support we could and soon after, he fell into an exhausted sleep.

"N'dugu," I asked some time later. "What are we going to do now?"

He looked at me, a light shining in his golden eyes. "Tomorrow, we will explore our new home. Everything is so new here. I just hope we have enough prey to keep us fed. I don't think the grazers from home migrate this far and I do not smell any great herds nearby. I also don't smell many predators."

"I am scared." I laid my head on my paws as memories flashed in my mind. "But Mother said it was good to be scared. I wonder if we will ever see her again."

N'dugu leaned against me, laying his head on my side. "I will protect you so you don't have to be scared. We are all together and together, we can do anything."

And I believed him. I closed my eyes and listened to the soft unfamiliar night sounds. There were no lions, no hyena, no elephants. Just insects and the wind rustling through the grass. Tomorrow would be a whole new adventure.

Chapter Seven: Tragedy

The next morning, we woke to unfamiliar surroundings. Suddenly, everything from the past few days came rushing back. We were in a new place! Part of me was scared but a bigger part was excited, reminding me of N'dugu from our younger days. Thinking of my older brother, and now my leader, I turned to find him. He and Soji sat solemnly next to Kana, who still slept curled into a ball. I cautiously approached.

"Is Kana still unwell?" I asked.

"Yes," N'dugu answered. "But we need to find food. Someone will have to stay with him while the other follows me into the grass."

Although my stomach grumbled in protest, my concern for Kana outweighed my desire for food. "I will stay with him. If you're able, bring something back for us."

"We will. Be safe, Sahara. Soji and I will be back before dark." He butted his head against mine and he and Soji disappeared into the grass.

I turned back to Kana who whimpered softly in his sleep. Trying to offer whatever comfort I could, I curled around him. To my relief, his whimpering stopped.

Several hours later, as the sun was starting its decent, Kana had still not roused from his sleep. Restless, I sat at the edge of the shelter that protected us and peered out, looking for any sign of N'dugu or Soji. At a sudden yelp from Kana, I turned and ran back to him. His eyes opened but he did not uncurl from his ball.

"Are you feeling any better?" I asked, dropping to my belly next to him.

"Not really," he groaned. "I wanted to go out and explore this new land with you all."

"You will," I reassured. "As soon as you are better."

"Thank-you, Sahara, for being such a great sister."

His words and tone unsettled me and I chuckled. What else was I supposed to do? "Thank-you for being such a great brother."

"He may not show it…" Kana continued as though I hadn't spoken. "…but N'dugu really looks up to you. Most of his decisions are either to make sure you stay safe or to prove to you he is worthy of being leader. Me and Soji, too. Maybe it is because you remind us so much of Mother."

"Kana, you're being silly. I'm no better than the rest of you."

"Maybe and maybe not." He opened his mouth and yawned, his jaw popping from the effort. "I love you, Sahara. Don't ever forget that." With his last words, he closed his eyes and drifted back off to sleep.

"I love you, too, silly." Although I meant for it to sound light, concern still etched my voice. What would make my gentle, loving brother say those things? I returned to my spot at the burrow opening and continued my vigil.

Luckily, I didn't have long to wait. It was not yet dark when I spotted N'dugu and Soji loping toward the shelter, each with a fat leg hanging from their jaws. I licked my lips and turned to Kana.

"Kana! We have food," I called.

But Kana did not even flinch. I tried to call again with the same result. N'dugu entered the shelter and dropped the shank at my feet then went to check on Kana.

Ignoring the gift, I turned to him. "He was awake a little while ago. We talked for a bit but he was saying some confusing things. He wouldn't wake up when I told him we had food."

Without looking at me, N'dugu said, "Go ahead and eat, Sahara. I will try and rouse him."

Not needing anymore prompting, I dug into the leg.

"Kana, brother," N'dugu said softly against Kana's ear. "You need to eat to regain your strength. I have to show you this new world and we need to get water soon."

Kana did not stir at N'dugu's words.

"Please, brother. Just a morsel."

Kana finally peeled back an eyelid and peered, unseeing, at N'dugu. "I just need a bit more rest," he whispered, almost too low for me to hear.

"Alright then. Until tomorrow."

Kana closed his eye again and drifted back off to sleep. N'dugu stared down at our brother with an agonized look in his eyes. I'd seen that look before, in Mother's eyes right before we lost Nahi. I forgot about my dinner and whimpered. N'dugu turned to me, erasing the pain in his eyes.

"Eat," he ordered. "Tomorrow we will explore this land."

Soji dropped his meat next to me and sat a few feet away. "Take this one as well, sister. It will spoil before Kana can rouse enough to eat it and there is plenty where it came from."

After finishing off the legs and dragging the leftovers away from the burrow, we all curled around Kana. Surprisingly, Soji cuddled closely to me. He was the most introverted of all my brothers but as we grew older, he began to act a lot like N'dugu. Soji is what I imagined our father looked like: tall, handsome, with the standard pebble-sized spots typical of most cheetah. His golden eyes saw more than we ever imagined. I came to realize he was an observer, analyzing the environment around him before acting, much different from out childhood days when he was nearly as rash as N'dugu and Kana.

His unusual behavior of snuggling up to me, as well as N'dugu's earlier action, had a rock-hard lump forming at the bottom of my stomach.

A crack of thunder woke me the next morning, followed by the heavy scent of rain on the breeze. The rains had returned to the plains. I jumped up and ran for the entrance to our burrow. Just above the hazy horizon, the sun struggled to clear the earth. Above, high in the sky were clouds as dark as pitch. On the other horizon were wide rain bands, threatening to blot out the newborn sun. I closed my eyes and breathed deeply the pure scent of ozone. Behind me, a whimper caught my ears. I turned to see both Soji and N'dugu looking down at an unnaturally still Kana. He had uncurled somewhat from his ball during the night and his legs tangled around themselves. The lump in my stomach returned and I slowly approached my baby brother.

"Kana?" I asked, impotently. "N'dugu, wake him up. He can not sleep this long."

N'dugu looked at me pitifully. "He will not wake up, Sahara. It is best we leave him to his eternal rest."

"What? No...he was talking just fine yesterday. He must wake up!" I butted my head against Kana's shoulder but the stiffened muscles barely moved. Whimpering, I lay next to him and just cried.

"We will stay here just a bit longer but then we need to move," N'dugu said, his voice full of the pain both me and Soji felt.

We all laid next to our lost brother, desperate to hold on to our memories of him. When the rains reached the burrow a few hours later, we left it, and our brother, behind. After moving several feet away, we turned as one and sat down, watching as the rains eroded the burrow and buried Kana. With nothing else to keep us there, we turned and headed further into our new home.

Chapter Eight: Sanctuary

The rains continued unabated for several hours with blinding forks of lightning streaking across the sky. The thunder that followed rumbled through the air and vibrated the ground. Occasionally, a bolt of lightning would hit nearby and the simultaneous crack of thunder had us dropping to the ground with our ears pulled against our heads. So heavy was the rain, we couldn't see more than a few feet in front of us. N'dugu turned to me and Soji, water running in rivulets down his nose.

"Let's find shelter," he shouted over the noise. "We'll not find anything to hunt today."

We nodded our agreement, already weary of the rain. Some time later we found a rock formation that allowed us some cover, although it was barely large enough for the three of us. Of course, chilled to the bone, we were okay with this. For the rest of the night we slept to the sound of rain, wind, and thunder.

The next morning the clouds had parted to reveal a drenched world. With stiff joints we crawled from our shelter. I stretched and yawned so widely my jaw popped. After giving my body a good shake, I looked around. Already, green shoots were peeking through the brown grass. Nature sure was amazing! I turned to greet my brothers and came face to face with a groggy Soji. His fur stuck up in all directions, making for a comical appearance. I couldn't help the laugh that bubbled up from my stomach. His golden eyes glared at me as he cocked his head.

"I don't know what you're laughing at," he smirked. "You look even worse than me."

That sobered me up and I worked franticly to get my fur back under control. My tongue couldn't reach my head so I had to use my paws. Satisfied that I was as groomed as I was going to get, I returned Soji's smirk. His grooming attempt was only half-hearted, leaving him with some places that were smooth and some that were still wild. I chuckled softly and went to find N'dugu.

Sitting on top of the rock formation, he stared out into the distance. Like Soji and I, his fur was mussed and sticking up at all angles. But N'dugu never bothered to groom it. He once said it was too long and troublesome. Being N'dugu, he was probably right.

I climbed the rocks to sit next to him. He was so deep in his thoughts that I doubt he even realized I was there. I turned my eyes to see what he was looking at. Far off into the distance was a mountain almost obscured by the early morning mist. Between it and our shelter was the most beautiful landscape I could ever remember seeing. A river wound its way through tall grasses and open savannah. Elephants, buffalo, and a few wildebeest meandered through the grasses, taking advantage of the early shoots. A bit closer to us was a herd of waterbuck, a creature I'd only ever heard of. Interspersed through them were oribi, an antelope similar to a gazelle. Closer to the mountain was a swath of thick trees that I imagined continued up onto the peak. I was speechless for several moments. At some point, Soji joined us and was just as enraptured as me and N'dugu.

"Can you believe this," I whispered, afraid of breaking the spell. "I wish Kana could have seen this."

"Kana is seeing this," N'dugu reassured. "He is now forever part of this land, in every seed that sprouts and animal that finds nourishment. We must not dwell on our loss but honor him by making this the best home we can."

"You are right, brother," Soji said. "As always, your wisdom puts everything into perspective."

N'dugu turned and climbed down the rocks. "Let us hunt before the rains return."

Without a word we followed him into the long grass.

The rest of the rainy season passed uneventfully. With so many different types of antelope, we had begun to hunt the waterbuck, the only other prey we could safely take down near the water. Although the grazers did migrate somewhat, we never had to go far to find food. It did give us the opportunity to further explore the land. Following the river, we discovered a great lake filled with hippos and crocodiles. Elephants played in water made crystalline by the rising and setting sun. We stayed near the lake for some time, soaking in the beauty and peace of it all. There were so many different kinds of animals, many of which we had only heard tales of, like the nyala and the eland, two types of antelope.

Not far from the lake was the beginnings of a great forest. Occasionally, the eyes of some unknown creature would peek out of the shadows. A part of me, the part most like N'dugu, wanted to go explore the deep recesses. But I knew it was not a wise decision. Leopards could live among those trees and I knew they would not hesitate to injure or kill me. So, I stayed near the lake and used my imagination.

Halfway into spring, while most of the herds were calving, we heard our first lion. We had just eaten and were sated and lazy, lounging on a few boulders and soaking up the heat from the sun. The golden orb had already begun its downward decent and a cool breeze was blowing off the lake. Without warning, the herds bolted into a stampede, startling us out of our stupor. We were far enough away not to be in danger but we knew only one thing would have the herds so panicked, and it wasn't us. That was when we heard it: the roar of a male lion. We turned our heads to the rear of the stampede and, just above the long grass we caught the flick of a tail.

Not much later, the lions had brought down an elderly wildebeest and began feeding. We counted nearly a dozen animals, although several appeared to be yearlings. N'dugu turned to me and Soji.

"We need to move," he said matter-of-factly. "We will follow the river so that we can be near water and prey. With luck, that is the only pride on these lands."

Like ghosts, we slipped into the tall grass and disappeared. Luckily, the lions never witnessed our departure. I doubted, at the time, they even knew we were there. In hindsight, however, I realize that, of course they knew we were there. Or at least that some big predator was there. What else would take down the prey we did? In any case, the lions did not bother us and we did not bother them. On our way downriver, we did hear a few hyena, probably following the lions as they are wont to do.

One evening, as we were making our way to our temporary shelter, I turned to N'dugu with a sudden realization.

"N'dugu," I said, softly. "Have you noticed what is missing from this new home of ours?"

"Many things are missing, Sahara," he said with infinite patience. "Can you be more specific?"

"There are no giraffes."

He stopped suddenly and I had to dance around him to keep from bumping into his side. Soji, following behind and out of earshot, did not notice N'dugu stopping and ran into his back end.

"Oomph…" Recovering quickly, Soji scanned the area for danger. "What is it, brother?"

"Sahara's right," he said, turning to face us. "There are no giraffe here. I never even noticed before. I wonder what else is different."

"I haven't seen any two-legs since we arrived," Soji contributed. "Maybe we are finally safe."

My mind had drifted a bit during the conversation and N'dugu, always alert, noticed my preoccupation. "What is it, Sahara?"

"I was just thinking of something Mother said when we were still cubs, back when Nahi was still alive. She said there would be a 'king' cheetah that would see our species out of the dark and into the light. He would be a savior and other cheetah would flock to him for safety and security. She seemed so sure that would be you" I turned to them. "I'd almost forgotten the story until Soji mentioned the two-legs. I think we are the only cheetah here. We can't even find mates. How are you going to save our species if we can't even save ourselves? What is the point to all of this?"

"All things in time, sister," N'dugu reassured me. "If Mother believed I was this savior, then I will be. Everything will work out in the end and some day, we will find our mates. In the meantime, we will continue to stick together because it is safer in numbers, especially in this strange place with no giraffe."

"I understand, brother." I bumped my head against his for a moment. "You know, when Mother said you would grow up to be wise, I laughed. I didn't believe her. But you really are wise. I'm glad you're my brother."

N'dugu laughed. "I was pretty reckless back then."

"Maybe," Soji contributed. "But your adventurous nature gave us the courage to face the world, especially after Nahi. We couldn't have gotten this far without you."

"Thanks, guys. I only wish I could have gotten Nahi and Kana this far as well."

"It's as you said, brother. All things in time." Soji butted N'dugu as well and then started off again to our shelter, the setting sun turning his form into a silhouette.

N'dugu and I followed quietly behind.

Chapter Nine: Wandering

Spring came to an end and the land began to dry
out, leaving the once vibrant grasses dry and brittle.
Although N'dugu had urged us to stay together, I felt
a pulling that I couldn't always ignore. I knew it was
instinct kicking in. Normally by now, I would have
already left my brothers in search of a mate and
territory of my own. But these weren't normal times
and I was nowhere near my childhood home. I also

knew that, despite my desire for a family of my own, there were no other cheetah in this strange, yet beautiful land. Even if I left my brothers, I would not find what my instincts were urging me to seek out. At times, I wondered, *What's the point in all of this if we are doomed to die out without providing the land with a future generation?*

Although N'dugu and Soji had to have noticed my absence, they never brought it up. I think they understood what I was going through. After all, we grew up without a father and Mother was only a few turn of the seasons older than I was now. Still, when I returned from my wanderings, N'dugu and Soji greeted me with purrs and butted heads as if I'd never left.

Near the end of summer, just a few weeks before the rains began, I found myself once again alone. It had been three moons since I'd seen my brothers, although I could sometimes still hear their chirps in the night if it was especially quiet. The sweltering heat simmered off the land creating waves of illusionary water. Panting, I took shelter beneath an old gnarled, leafless tree. It provided some relief from the sun but the heat was still intense enough to cause my chest to rise rapidly in an effort to cool my overheated body.

I dozed, my ears flicking away the biting insects buzzing around me, when a small commotion drew my attention. Tiny yelps and growls had me lifting my head. Several yards away were three tiny jackal pups fighting over a bone. I watched their fight for some time, mesmerized by their play. That deep recess inside me that took me from my brothers called out to them. Where were their parents? Without thinking, I rose to my feet. Before taking a step, however, reason returned.

What are you going to do with them? I chided myself. It wasn't like I could keep them and raise them as my own.

As I watched, a grown wild dog came up to them. Once again, my instincts stepped in. I wanted to stop the wild dog from hurting the pups. I watched, amazed as the pups ran up to her and began licking her jaws. It appeared someone had already adopted them.

I laid back on my belly and watched the unusual family. The wild dog was very doting and she scanned the area for danger, her satellite ears shifting to and fro. Without warning, she left the pups who were once again fighting over the bone, moving several feet away. Suddenly, two adult jackals ran up to the pups and regurgitating half eaten meat. *So, they are the pups' parents. I wonder, then, where do you fit in?*

I turned to the wild dog who sat contentedly watching the family. Such curious behavior had me questioning everything I thought I understood about the world. Then, I remembered where I was. Nothing about this place was ordinary. I had never seen such a diverse ecosystem living in harmony before. Watching the wild dog gave me hope for the future. As if she could feel me staring at her, the wild dog turned her head and met my stare, almost as if she'd known I was there the whole time. A moment later she stood and trotted away.

To my surprise, she looked expectantly over her shoulder at me, beckoning me to follow. My curiosity piqued, and a desire for companionship had me getting to my feet to follow. We traveled for a long time before she stopped. I think she wanted me far from her adopted family. As the sun began its descent, shooting rainbow rays across the sky, she finally stopped and lay on her belly. I'd followed several feet behind and moved to lay next to her. We sat in comfortable silence for many minutes before she spoke.

"I have never seen your kind here before but I have heard stories from long ago," she began. "Truthfully, I'm surprised you have returned."

"Why?" I asked, aching to hear her story.

"Because it is not safe for you here." She turned to me with sad eyes.

Her words shocked me to my core. We'd lived in this new home for nearly a whole turn of the seasons and the only threat we found was a pride of lions who had kept to themselves. What was this danger she spoke of?

"Why do you say that?" I asked, needing to understand her.

"The cheetah didn't just disappear. They were killed, some by lions. But most were killed by the hunters who walk on two legs. Not just the cheetah, but most of the animals in this paradise."

"But, there are countless animals here." I began to question her motives. Maybe she was just trying to scare me so that me and my brothers would leave.

"It was a long time ago, before I was even born. And I have seen many turns of the seasons. Would you like to hear the story from the beginning?"

"Yes," I answered, shifting to get more comfortable.

"This land was once a hidden paradise with one of the richest and diverse ecosystems in all of Africa. There were animals here that did not exist anywhere else on the earth and others, such as the oribi that had the densest populations ever seen. There were lions, leopards, rhinos, hyena, cheetah, and wild dogs, all in abundance. Hundreds of different species of birds and reptiles graced the sky and land. The food was plentiful and the land itself was lush and beautiful. Then the hunters came.

"From the stories passed down through my ancestors, the hunters didn't even come for the land originally. The came to hunt each other. I remember thinking how unbelievable that was. What species hunts their own so viciously?"

"In my limited encounters with two legs, I found them to be a conundrum. It doesn't surprise me they would hunt each other for sport."

"That they did and this paradise was right in the middle of it all. The hunters scorched the land and began hunting the animals. Sometimes they killed for food, sometimes for sport. They used sticks that shot out fire and cracked the air like thunder. Many animals died, most of those who lived here. It was a desolate place, ravaged by a war we wanted no part of.

"Some years ago, long before my birth, the hunters left and the land began to heal. Some of the animals returned on their own. Others were brought in by other two-legs to boost native populations, like the hippos, elephants, and lions. Some, like yourself, were brought in to reintroduce your species. Unfortunately, no wild dogs have returned and I am the last of my family."

"I am very sorry for your loss," I said, lowering my head. "It must be very lonely. Back home, we often observed wild dog packs. There were too many to count."

"I am finding my place," she said with only a hint of sadness. "My adopted family has given me much joy and I have made other unlikely friends."

"If the land is recovering, why do you fear for my brothers and I?"

"The hunters did not stay gone. Sometimes, deep in the night, they slip back in and kill certain animals, mostly the elephants and big cats. Your spotted coat is a prize to them. And I have seen your unique brother once. He is especially in danger. If the hunters see him, they will stop at nothing to possess his pelt."

"That's terrible!" I fought a bout of nausea at her words.

"It is worse for the elephants. Some of the old matriarchs were alive when the hunters first came. They remember the reign of terror that followed and watched in horror as many of their kin were slaughtered for their tusks."

I couldn't say anything and we simply laid there in silence for many minutes. I took in the magnificence around me made golden by the descending sun. The water glittered like liquid gold, broken only by the occasional fish or water fowl. Somewhere off in the distance, a hippo surface, blowing a mist of water vapor into the air.

"If I can give you some advice," she said, breaking the silence. "Keep to the middle of the land, near the lake or close to the forest where you can quickly hide. The lions frequent there but the hunters do not like to travel too deeply into our territory. And the hunters are much more dangerous than the lions."

"Thank-you…uh…"

"M'vita. And you're welcome. I really hope to see you again and maybe even young ones one day."

"Thanks, M'vita. I'm Sahara. And I hope for the same for you."

We rose to our feet, nodded to each other, and went our separate ways. I made my way home as quickly as I could without exhausting myself, desperately needing the company and comfort of my brothers. I knew I was getting close when I heard N'dugu and Soji's chirps. My relief was felt in my answering chirps and they came out to meet me. Together, we made our way back to our home.

Chapter Ten: Close Encounters

After sharing M'vita's story with N'dugu and Soji, we decided to move closer to the lake. We knew we had to be vigilant, both because of the lions who were patrolling the area and because the rains would be returning soon. As it was, much of the herds stayed near the lake since it was the best source of water and the grass was still relatively green. This was why the lions were there. Once the rains came, however, the plain would flood and those nearest would need to move to higher ground. Still, we were confident if we stayed closer to the main river that fed the lake, we could still hunt without causing a problem for the lions.

The next few weeks, we hunted and slept constantly on alert. While we didn't really see the lions during the day, we knew they were there. At night, the male would roar for all hours, bringing back unpleasant memories from our childhood. I wished we could go back to the time before I met M'vita, when we thought we were safe in our new world.

One night, perhaps a week or so after arriving at our temporary shelter, the lions ran a night hunt. They came perilously close to where we slept and the agonizing cries of their dying prey kept us from sleep. The next day, we moved further downriver. The prey was thinner and our choices more limited. The water was also ripe with crocodiles. Simply bending down for a drink was to risk one's life.

After a second unsuccessful hunt, Soji and I collapsed in the shade of a tree. We took in deep breaths, trying to both cool our overheated bodies and to slow our pounding hearts. N'dugu sat off to the side. He panted as well but he did not run as far as we did. By the time he joined the chase, it was clear the antelope would outmaneuver us.

My stomach grumbled in protest. As if it could hear me and had a mind of its own, Soji's stomach shared the sentiment, adding its own grumble. I looked at Soji and then turned to N'dugu. His back was to us as he stared off at the agitated herd.

"N'dugu, brother," I pleaded. "What are we going to do? We can't miss another meal. I'm too exhausted to run anymore."

"I know, sister," he answered, keeping his eyes on the herd. "The lions have forced us away from the best hunting grounds. The terrain here isn't ideal for our speed."

Without another word, he left Soji and me and disappeared into the grass. I looked at Soji with a worried expression. He just shrugged his shoulders, as confused as I. With no energy, I laid my head on the hard ground and closed my eyes. Sleep engulfed me almost before my lids were completely closed.

I woke up some time later to a thump near my head. Startled, I jumped to my feet. Unfortunately, my lack of food left me slightly dizzy and I swayed before getting my feet under me. Once my eyes focused, I spied what had wakened me. N'dugu stood before me looking at the hunk of meat and bone at my feet. Before I thought to even say thank-you, I dived into it. I barely registered Soji with his own meat, nearly devoured already.

"If we hurry, there may be some left," N'dugu said. "Supposing the scavengers haven't found it yet."

Eating quickly, we finished our meal and followed N'dugu to the rest of the carcass. Luckily, he'd managed to hide it in a way that no scavengers had yet found it. It was a very fresh kill and we all ate our fill. After that, hunting became easier. A few days later, the rains returned.

The rainy season always amazed me, it didn't matter how many times I witnessed it. It gave me hope that one day, the cheetah would come back as miraculously as the dead grasses and plains. If nature could do that every year, could she not also bring back the animals? After all, everything is a circle. The grazers eat the grass, the predators eat the grazers, and when the predators die, they return to the earth that feeds the grass. You can not have one without the other.

With the rains came the need to leave our temporary home. It did not take long for the river to flood its bank and everything around it. We moved further north out of the way of the flooding. While there, we found a new part of the territory we had not yet discovered. It proved a very fruitful discovery. The terrain was perfect for cheetah with wide open spaces where we could utilize our speed.

Like every rainy season, we took advantage of the abundance of prey, eating our fill to regain the strength lost during the dry season. This year, the rains did not last as long as usual and the grazers birthed earlier. This provided us with a bounty and, for a while, we forgot about lions and two-leg hunters.

A couple weeks into spring, we had brought down a large waterbuck. In fact, it was the largest we had ever managed to bring down and it was only through sheer luck we came across it.

It was sequestered among a large herd of other waterbuck who were feeding on the fresh green sprouts. We were actually looking at the oribi for a meal. Without any particular reason, the herd bolted, running for the water. The old waterbuck was bumped and fell onto its side.The bump wasn't even that hard and it drew our attention away from the oribi. It struggled to regain its footing and that's when we noticed a broken foot. The animal was lame! We wasted no time running over to it and ended its suffering.

So eager were we to grab the easy meal, we didn't even stop to think of what had caused the animals to run in the first place. Without the lion pride nearby, we had grown complacent. Savoring our kill we dug in with abandon.

A great roar sounded just over my shoulder and something much bigger than me plowed into me. I regained my feet quickly and turned to my adversary. The lion towered over me, his great mane fanning around his head. Huge canines snapped inches from my face. I ducked low and pulled my ears back, snarling back at him. But my snarls were like those of a kitten compared to the great beast. He was not fooled. I spared a fraction of a second to seek out my brothers.

They, too, faced off against an opponent. Soji had a large female breathing down his neck and N'dugu squared off with another male even bigger then mine. I chirped and turned to flee. I could see more lions coming from my periphery. N'dugu and Soji were in agreement but the lions would not let us leave so easily. We had to back away to protect our flanks, giving the lions ample room to swipe at us.

One hit caught me in my shoulder and I was slammed into the ground. I cried out in fear and pain while rolling back up to my feet. The lion was faster and pinned me beneath him. I kicked out with my hind legs, raking his underbelly. It was enough to throw him off me and I turned and fled. I briefly noticed N'dugu and Soji escaping their fights as well.

My lion refused to let me go so easily and swiped at my hip as I fled. I yelped and stumble but managed to regain my balance before he could hit me again. The brute chased me all the way into the trees. My smaller size gave me the advantage in the dense forest and I finally eluded him. Only now, I was in the dark forest that had always fascinated and scared me. Already, I could hear the deafening noise of birds, monkeys, and other creatures I could only guess at.

I slowly made my way through the trees, attempting to circumnavigate the lions and find my brothers. During my walk, my mind whirled. The lions who attacked us were not the ones from the lake. That pride only had one male. Which meant there was another pride of lions to watch out for and me and my brothers were caught between the two.

A sudden movement to my right caught my attention and I snapped my head in that direction. I couldn't get a clear sight, only an impression of its large size. I thought I saw stripes, like a zebra but we had yet to see any of the equine creatures anywhere in this new land. And besides, zebra don't live in the forest. Taking it for a trick of the light, I turned back around and quickened my pace from the forest.

Once I cleared the trees, I looked back to our kill. A pride, even bigger than the last feasted on the carcass. Truly, we were lucky to get out alive. I heard the chirps of my brothers some distance north of me and I ran to catch up. I hadn't even realized my hip was bleeding until I found my brothers and they began to fuss over me. Actually, I was somewhat embarrassed by the fact that I had injuries but they seemed unscathed by the encounter. After a good grooming and a night's rest, I felt a lot better.

Still, N'dugu told me to stay in the shelter until my leg healed completely. He would bring me food when they hunted again.

Luckily for me, it was calving season and finding vulnerable young was almost too easy. For the next few days, either N'dugu or Soji would bring me a calf to help rebuild my strength. It didn't take long for the injury to close up and soon, I was back on my feet and good as new. But lions weren't our only worry. We would soon find out the true meaning of fear and loss.

Chapter Eleven: Broken

The flood waters and lions pushed us further north then we had ever been before. The landscape changed somewhat, flattening out into a wide expanse of land dotted with trees and rivers. Off into the distance we could see the tightly clustered trees marking the beginning of a forest. The herds were spread out with more room to graze. In truth, it more resembled our home than any other part of this new world. There were outcroppings of rock perfect for observing our new home and we took advantage of them.

One morning, a couple of weeks after reaching our destination, I lay sprawled across a relatively flat rock taking in the view around me. The sun had just crested the horizon behind me, bathing the world in its golden glow. Dew drops glistened like millions of diamonds on the grasses and tiny flowers stretched for as far as the eye could see. Interspersed throughout these flowers were grazers: antelope of all kinds and sizes, a few wildebeest and buffalo, and almost hidden save for their tails, warthogs. In the sky, hundreds of birds flew this way and that, changing their flight direction without rhyme or reason like waves on water.

Far off, a herd of elephants meandered their way to the river. I had always been amazed at their strong family units. M'vita's words came back to me suddenly and my heart ached for those matriarchs who lived during the time of the hunters. If I could have, I would have liked to hear their stories from that time. I would have liked to ask them if they were around when the cheetah still lived in this land.

As I was lost in my reverie, N'dugu and Soji joined me on my rock, each laying down on either side of me. Together, we relished the peaceful moment. The comfort that my brothers brought me was unlike any other in the world and I silently thanked them for staying by my side. I knew that someday soon, instinct would win and we would be parted for good. Little did I know that a worser fate would find us first.

When the dry season returned, we traveled farther away from the lake and decided to follow one of its rivers instead, moving west along its banks. N'dugu knew it was a risk. The further from the large body of water, the less prey we would find. His hope was that there was more than one lake, since there were so many rivers. It was possible that a different lake would have no lions patrolling it. I think he was also hoping to find more cheetah. His drive to find a mate was even higher than mine.

The further west we traveled, the bigger the mountain in the distance became. We began to make out huge swaths of forest covering it nearly to the peak and spilling out around its feet. We skirted this forest, having no reason to enter its dark recesses. Our prey became scarcer, as we feared but the open terrain allowed for easier hunting. More importantly, we did not encounter any competition, no lions or hyena.

One afternoon, as the sun beat relentlessly down on the earth, a large antelope slowly made its way passed where we lounged. Ordinarily, we would not have paid the buck any mind. It was far too hot for a chase, especially if it ended in failure and the buck was really too large an animal for us to bring down anyway. However, its slow, careful pace seemed off and we watched as it tried to make its way to the river which, by now, was filled with eager crocodiles. He never made it to the water. Without warning, he stumbled and never regained his feet.

I looked to my brothers curiously. An unspoken agreement passed between us and as one, we rose to our feet. In the back of my mind, I still believed the animal would gain his feet and bolt for the water so I approached him carefully. My brothers, in the same frame of mind, followed my lead. When we reached the buck, he lay on his side, panting heavily. A small hole pierced his flank and a macabre red flower blossomed from it, sending red tendrils down his leg and into the grass. Although the injury didn't look that serious, the trail of blood the buck left told a different story. I'd never seen such a wound and knew it wasn't created by any predator I knew of.

The buck knew we stood near him; he could both see and smell us but he was too exhausted to fight any longer. I knew it would only be moments before he succumbed to his wounds. N'dugu, realizing the same thing, ended the poor creature's suffering.

Never one to miss an opportunity, we ate our fill that day.

As we made our way back to our rock, the hairs on the back of my neck stood up. I stopped suddenly and looked around. Something was out there, watching us. Soji, noticing my abrupt pause, turned and chirped.

"Is everything alright, sister?" he asked, watching me curiously.

"I don't know," I answered, my eyes still scanning the plains. "Something doesn't feel right."

Concerned, Soji walked over to me and began his own scan. "I don't see anything out of the ordinary."

"Nor I, but I know something is there. The wound on that buck wasn't normal. What kind of animal would do that?"

Soji shrugged his shoulders helplessly. "Come, we must catch up to N'dugu. The sooner we get to shelter, the sooner whatever is out there will move on." He bumped my shoulder playfully and nipped my ear.

"What are you, a cub?" I teased, bumping him back. I really hoped he was right. Together we stretched our long legs and jogged to catch up to our older brother.

"Am I going to have to separate you two?" N'dugu asked playfully. Really, it amazed me what he saw when we didn't think he noticed anything at all! Soji and I just chuckled.

True to his word, the uncomfortable feeling I had was gone by the next morning. Soji lay beside me asleep as I yawned loudly.

"Feeling better?" he asked, apparently not as asleep as I'd thought.

"Yeah, actually. Thanks for cheering me up yesterday."

"What are big brothers for?" He rolled onto his belly and yawned as well, stretching his long legs out in front of him.

I know I really shouldn't have. It was childish and immature but I really couldn't help myself. And besides, it was only a little push. Unfortunately, Soji was still stretching when my shoulder pushed against him and he yelped and tumbled from the rocks. Luckily, he landed on his feet but the glare he shot at me said I wouldn't get off so lucky. Laughing, I leapt from the stones and he made to come after me. His eyes were twinkling with mischief so I knew he wasn't really angry. That didn't mean I wanted him to catch me.

An urgent, high pitched chirping stopped us in our tracks. We snapped our heads in the direction of the sound. Something was wrong and N'dugu was sounding an alert. Soji and I swiveled our heads around looking for danger but could see nothing out of the ordinary. We cautiously made our way to where we last heard N'dugu.

That was when I felt it again, the sinister feeling from the day before. It was such a powerful, threatening aura that even Soji felt it and he turned fearful eyes to me.

"Run, Sahara!" and without another word we shot off across the plains.

N'dugu leapt over a log and joined us. "We must separate to confuse them," he panted.

"What is it?" I asked.

"I don't know but I think it killed that buck yesterday. Go different directions. We'll meet up again near the high rock. Be careful!"

Whimpering, I split off to the right. Soji continued straight and N'dugu turned left. A crack of thunder exploded through the air, sending birds shooting into the sky. Another crack followed and then all was silent.

I managed to reach the high rock and immediately turned to find my brothers. After a few moments, N'dugu joined me. We waited impatiently for Soji to join us. Minutes passed but there was no sign of our brother. Fear filled my belly and my previous meal threatened to leave in the way it entered.

"N'dugu?" I whimpered. "Where is Soji? Shouldn't he have made it here by now?"

N'dugu didn't answer. He stared off into the distance with a look of mixed pain and anger burning in his eyes. "Come, we can not stay here."

"We can't leave without Soji," I cried. "N'dugu, I can't lose another brother."

He sighed and lowered his head. "We will go back but keep to the shadows. Whatever that thing is may still be out there."

I nodded and followed behind him in silence. It didn't take long to reach the place I'd last seen Soji. At first, we didn't see anything. The plains were eerily quiet and still. Then, I saw movement from the corner of my eye. A two-legs stood from the brush, the body of a cheetah draped over its shoulders. Although the hunter was quite far away, I didn't need to be any closer to realize the cheetah was Soji. N'dugu, drawn to my cry, witnessed what I did. Pulling me to the ground beneath him, he blocked the sight from my view. In mere minutes, the two-legs disappeared into the trees, taking half my heart with it.

Chapter Twelve: Despair

The loss of Soji broke something in both me and
N'dugu. For me, losing another sibling left a vacant
hole inside, especially since there were no other
cheetah in this new land to fill it. After Kana died, Soji
became more protective of me and we built a bond
on both mutual suffering and a strong desire to live.
He made me laugh when all I wanted to do was cry.

With him, I could still pretend to be a cub, protected and loved.

For N'dugu, Soji's loss was so much more. N'dugu held himself responsible because he felt that it was his duty to not only protect his siblings but the entire cheetah species. Soji's death was the ultimate failure for him. If he couldn't protect his own siblings, how was he going to protect the rest of the cheetah in Africa? He withdrew into himself and rarely spoke unless absolutely necessary. With just the two of us, he took his vigil over me to suffocating levels.

One night, just a few days after Soji's death, I started awake from a nightmare. N'dugu sat next to me staring off into nothing. At first, I thought I had woken him, only to realize he had never slept. During the day, he stayed close to me and wouldn't let me leave his sight. When we hunted, he let me eat first while he kept watch. Without Soji, we needed to hunt smaller prey who were faster than the larger antelope. I could hear his stomach grumble as

I fed and I ate quickly so that he could before the scavengers came.

While I appreciated his presence, his protectiveness began to chafe against my desire for freedom. Still, I understood and respected his need to see to my safety. Because of this, I endured it all with tried patience. However, the silence was not something I could live with. Throughout my whole life, all four summer's worth, I had been surrounded by the playful banter of my siblings. As time went on, and I lost one after another, the banter turned more serious, but there was always someone to talk to, always someone to pour my insecurities out to. Even N'dugu was open to conversation when we were together. But after Soji's death, he wouldn't speak to me.

I tried once to talk to him, to relieve some of the pain burdening me but he didn't seem to pay attention at all. So wrapped up in his own pain, he failed to see how much I needed him. With no one else to talk to, my pain and anger festered within me until one day, it exploded.

N'dugu once again sat staring off into nothing, his back ramrod straight in front of me. It was mid-day and sweltering but it didn't seem to phase him at all. I watched him in all of his magnificent glory. In another time, I would have appreciated his beauty, the glistening silkiness of his fur and obsidian markings so different from mine. On this day, however, I was furious. Not so much with him. Just angry in general.

"Brother, would you please talk to me?" I pleaded. My only answer was the rustle of wind through the trees. "I can not stand the silence any longer." Still he did not move.

Without another word, I rose to my feet and started walking away. Even without looking back, I knew he followed. My anger exploded out of me and I turned on him, snarling and swiping a paw at his face. Startled, he jumped back. A single chirp left his throat and that tiny response set me off again. After all we'd been through, the only thing he could give me was a single, pitiful chirp! I lunged for him and threw him to the ground, despite his much bigger size. I pounded away at him, raking my claws across that silky fur and vulnerable underbelly. He did not fight back and after a few minutes, I realized why. He wanted to be punished for his failure and he felt that my anger was justified. I immediately stopped and jumped back.

Chagrined, I lowered my ears. "I'm sorry, brother. I did not mean to take my anger out on you."

He rolled onto his belly and stared at me.

When it became obvious he wouldn't respond, I continued. "I'm going off on my own. It is passed time I did so and staying together isn't healthy for either one of us."

This seemed to get his attention and he rose to his feet. "Please don't go," he said, sadness filling his eyes. "I don't want to be alone."

"N'dugu, we are cheetah, not lions. The way we have been living, the way this place has forced us to live, is not natural. We are solitary creatures. I have been fighting this for too long and I'm tired."

He whimpered and lowered his head. I knew what he was thinking. Male cheetah, brothers, often stayed together for life but with the loss of Soji, N'dugu was well and truly alone. Looking at him, he looked like the lost cub from our youth.

"We are still siblings, N'dugu. It isn't like we'll never see one another again."

"How am I supposed to save the cheetah all by myself? There is no one left here, save you and I."

"Mother said it was prophesied that you would save the cheetah. That means something will happen to make that possible. Who knows what the future holds. I love you, brother, and I believe in you."

I rubbed my head against his neck one last time. Whimpering, he returned the affection. Even though I was leaving him, I knew I would see him again.

"I love you, too, Sahara. Be safe out there."

I pulled back and nodded. I was glad to see the spark of determination return to his eyes. With a flick of my tail, I turned and trotted off. My destination was southeast, back toward the lake. I knew the lions were there but it was also the best place to find impala, the only prey I could really hunt on my own. Besides, it was where my instinct led me.

The next several weeks passed peacefully. On the one hand, it was strange not having my brothers to talk to. On the other, I think N'dugu's silence had conditioned me to being on my own. The quiet didn't really bother me. It did give me a lot of time to think, and heal. While I still missed Soji, and my anger toward the two-legs still burned, the emptiness inside began to fill up with the wonder of my world. The rains returned and I watched, as I did every year, as the land once again came to life. During a break in the rain, I lounged on a rock, soaking up the sun. A noise to my right had me turning my head in that direction.

M'vita sat in the damp grass looking up at me. Her large ears flicked at the biting flies that multiplied with the rains and her obsidian eyes bore into me.

"I am glad to see that you are still alive," she said. "But you are alone. How are your brothers?"

A twinge of pain crossed my face and, realizing what it meant, she opened her mouth to speak. Before she could, I said, "N'dugu is well but we lost Soji to the hunters."

She lowered her head a moment before looking back up. 'I am sorry for your loss."

"How have you been?"

"Content. The little ones are off finding families of their own so it is a little lonely right now. However..." Her words trailed off and she looked away.

"What it is?"

"I think there may be a pack of dogs nearby."

I jumped up and leapt from the rock. The cool, wet grass chilled the pads of my feet and I shivered. My sudden movement startled M'vita and she jumped back.

"Sorry," I said, shrugging my shoulders. "Have you seen them?"

"Not yet, but I can smell their scent and sometimes I hear them."

"That's great! Are you going to try to find them?"

"I don't know. I have been on my own for so long it feels kind of strange being among my own kind again. And what if they don't accept me?"

"This could be your only chance to find others like you. I think you should go for it."

"Maybe you're right. Good luck, Sahara. Remember to watch your back. If the wild dogs are returning, maybe the cheetah will, too."

"Thanks, and good luck to you, too."

I watched in silent amazement as she disappeared over the ridge. Wild dogs were returning! Spring really was an amazing time. I looked around me again at the beauty unfolding before my eyes. *Maybe she is right.* With the wild dogs' return and Mother's prophesy, it seemed very likely that it was just a matter of time before cheetah once again graced this land of paradise. As if in agreement, a herd of elephants trumpeted off a chorus from the lake. I chuckled at the playful nature of the behemoths. Life was an amazing thing.

Chapter Thirteen: Confrontation

With the end of the rain came an abundance of food for both predator and prey alike. Despite this abundance, I still had to abandon a kill occasionally, mostly to the heckling hyenas that usually followed the lions. It didn't take the lions long to figure out that I was in their territory, however. Mostly, I stayed on the outskirts, hunting the prey that moved further away from the lake.

By the time the rains ended, I had become used to being alone. In fact, I found a strange comfort in it. I finally found where I fit in this world and even the herds seemed to have a grudging respect for me. I hunted only what I needed and left them in peace the rest of the time. In hindsight, I don't think the herds even knew what to make of me and my brothers when we first arrived. It was as if they'd never even seen a cheetah before, which was most likely the case from what M'vita had told me. Now, however, they knew what I was and what I could do. Also, I was alone instead of in a hunting group like the lions.

As the spring progressed, I would catch fleeting glimpses of N'dugu at the edge of the horizon and smell his scent as I walked my territory. I know it was his way of making sure I was well and I was okay with that.

One evening in late spring, I heard the yelping of many dogs. They were still some ways off but their yips and barks echoed through the air. I turned toward the direction and caught just a glimpse of the pack running through the grasses, their white-tufted tails wagging in the air. I imagined I saw M'vita among their numbers but they were too far away to tell for sure. I sighed and lay my head across my paws. *Someday...*I thought.

Summer came early that year and was the fiercest I'd ever felt it. Many of the rivers shrank to mere trickling streams or dried up altogether. The water that was available was murky and filled to bursting with eager and cranky crocodiles. Even the fish suffered, many dying in the rivers-turned-mud. Their gills gasped in the open air as the fish suffocated. For some, this was a smorgasbord, a great variety of fish to dine on without the wasted effort of hunting for it. The waterfowl dodged the snapping jaws of crocodiles for the promise of an easy meal.

I worried about N'dugu since he relied so heavily on the rivers for survival. My worry, however, was short lived when I realized that I, too, was in danger.

Late one evening, the hierarchy of the lions changed. The great roaring of male lions startled me from my sleep. From what I could tell, three lions were battling for control of the pride. The sounds from the battle sent chills up my spine. I remember seeing one of these battles as a cub and the brutality of it gave me nightmares for days afterword. Some time later, we came across the old male that lost, his bones picked clean by the vultures. I feared what this change would mean for me.

By morning, the fight was over and two lions roared a message that could be heard for miles: "We are the new kings of this land!" I wondered if the other male survived. Pushing the thought passed me, I made my way to a stream I'd found a few days prior. After slaking my thirst, I left to find food.

Although I usually skirted the lake in search of prey, the dry summer forced me to move closer. The herds, those that stayed in the area, kept close to the only reliable water source and what was left of the green grasses. If I wanted to eat, I would have to follow them. As I moved closer to the water, however, I found the pride of lions lounging between me and the herds. There was no way for me to get passed them without them seeing. Despite the distracted males who were busy asserting their dominance, I knew the lionesses were alert as ever, especially given that many had young cubs hidden beneath their bellies.

I ignored my grumbling stomach and turned back toward the plains. I would just have to find something further out.

Three days passed before I found a small herd of impala exhausted by the heat and lack of water. They were crossing through my territory on the way to the lake. By this time, I was absolutely famished and nearly too weak to chase anything down. Still, I pulled all my reserve energy for a single run. If I couldn't bring something down, I would most likely starve. I ignored the gnawing pain in my stomach and crouched low behind the herd. When I was close enough, I shot out from the grass and sprinted straight for the herd.

It took them a moment before they noticed me, allowing me a few extra seconds to close the distance. The dirt kicked up by my feet drew their attention and they scattered, even before they realized what was actually coming for them. They were fast, nearly as fast as me. But they were also exhausted. After a short chase, one of them stumbled and fell to the ground. I didn't waste a moment and lunged for it. The whole thing lasted less than a minute.

Although I had brought the impala down and killed it, I was too exhausted to feed right away. My heart pounded and my chest rose and fell rapidly as I tried to regain my breath. The unrelenting sun bore down on me, making it even more difficult to regain an ounce of strength. I glanced up at the vultures, always ready for an unattended meal.

Before I could savor my victory and fill my empty stomach, a lion raced out of the grass, fresh wounds crisscrossing his face. The old male snarled and swiped his huge paw at me, trying to chase me away from my prey. It was the ousted male from the pride. *So he did survive.*

I was too hungry to surrender my meal. I knew what walking away from it would mean. I also knew what staying meant. The male was much bigger than me. He was also hungry and exhausted. I doubted he'd eaten since being banished from the pride. My hunger caused me to ignore the logical part of my brain, the part that told me, as my mother and brothers so often did, to abandon the prey to a bigger or stronger opponent and live to hunt another day. I was not confident I could find the strength to hunt again and even if I did, who's to say the lion wouldn't take it again?

So, I stood my ground. I lowered my body and ears and snarled at the lion. At first, he almost laughed at my attempt.

"Don't you know how this works, little one?" he rasped, condescendingly. "You cannot fight me. And I don't particularly want to kill you."

"You are too weak to kill me," I shot back, baiting him. "Go get your own prey. You male lions are so dependent on your females you have forgotten how to hunt."

I probably should have kept my mouth shut but, like I said, I wasn't thinking logically. The lion roared in anger and charged me, knocking me to the ground.

"Do not speak of things you could never understand," he hissed.

His heavy weight pressed into me as his jaws snapped inches from my face. I pushed up with all four of my feet, trying to dislodge him but he was too heavy and I too weak from hunger. He shifted slightly to get a better angle of my throat. Panicked, I used all the strength I had to push while biting the leg nearest my head. He roared and leapt away.

I stared into his vacant eyes. This was an animal with nothing left to lose. He'd lost his family, his territory, his home. Most likely, he would spend the rest of his life alone. My little existence meant nothing to him. I looked back at my neglected prey and realized I would have to leave it. Before I could move, the lion, perhaps misunderstanding my intentions, lunged at me. I was unprepared when his massive teeth sank into my thigh. I cried out as his top and bottom canines came together inside of my leg. With a mighty shake of his ragged mane, he pulled me to the ground. I knew then that I was going to die. There was no surviving this encounter.

My head dropped to the ground in utter defeat just before a great commotion erupted above me. Biting back the pain of my suddenly released leg, I looked up to see N'dugu and the lion in a life or death battle. The lion towered over N'dugu but my brother was well fed and rested. Admitting defeat, the lion turned and disappeared through the grass. N'dugu turned concerned eyes to me.

"Are you crazy?" he scolded, bending down to try and help me up. "How many times have you been told not to fight lions?"

I whimpered and turned away. My leg felt like a fire raged within it and I could not put any weight on it. I turned to see blood flowing freely from a massive wound, leaving a gruesome puddle on the ground. Bits of bone protruded through the flesh and fur. Even though N'dugu had saved me from the lion, I would not be able to hunt for a while. I was as good as dead.

N'dugu sighed and I turned to him. "I'm sorry, brother. I was just so hungry."

"It's alright. Let's get you cleaned up."

I looked longingly back at my prey, the cause for all of this. Sighing again, N'dugu picked up the impala. Luckily, it was small enough for him to carry in his mouth. Leaning against his shoulder, we made our way back to my little stream. I laid down in the warm water with my bad leg under me. The water stung and washed away some of the debris. After a few minutes, the wound became numb and I was able to eat.

N'dugu stayed with me over the next few days, making sure I was going to be okay. However, on the third day, it became obvious I was anything but alright. My body burned with fever and my leg festered and oozed. I could do nothing but lay on my side and pant.

Chapter Fourteen: Dire Circumstances

I slipped in and out of consciousness, hovering somewhere in between. In my delirium, I remember seeing N'dugu pacing in front of me. Sometimes, he would leave my sight altogether and I would fear, for just a moment, he had left me to my fate. Every now and then he would come up to me and bump his head against mine in our signature show of affection.

When I didn't respond, he would lick my face and whimper.

On the night of the third day, he lay next to me, his body flush against mine. Despite the heat of the day, my fever left me chilled and I shivered uncontrollably. N'dugu used his body heat to try to calm my shivering. I found some measure of comfort as he rested his chin on my shoulder. In one of my lucid moments, I listened as he pleaded with me.

"Sahara," he cried softly, probably thinking me asleep. "You must get better. I don't want to be all alone. You are my strength. You always have been. In truth, you were all of our strengths. If it wasn't for you, Kana and Soji wouldn't have lived as long as they did. In the end, I know they were happy with their lives. It was all because of you, sister. You gave us purpose. If you leave me now, what will my purpose be? How can I go on all alone in this strange world, the last surviving cheetah in paradise? Please get better."

I drifted off after that. I'd wanted to reassure him but I was too weak to speak. My dreams that night were as inconsistent as my waking hours. Nothing had form. They were simply filled with a kaleidoscope of colors that left me dizzy and more exhausted than before.

The next morning I woke to a commotion near me. N'dugu snarled at something I could not see. Instinct had his body set to flee but familial responsibility kept him near me. I struggled to lift my head to see what he faced off against. If it were a predator, I was as good as dead.

"Shh," came a strange and alien voice. "We are not going to hurt you."

I couldn't understand the words but the tone was soft and soothing. It left a feeling of calm within me. N'dugu, however, stood his ground. He lowered his body, pulled back his ears, and raised the long hairs along his neck and back. Pulling his lips back, he hissed and flashed his sharp canines at whoever it was approaching.

"We need to get him away from her or it will be too late," came the strange voice.

N'dugu yelped and tried to flee. He did not get far before he stumbled and fell. I whimpered, wishing for all the world I could save my brother. Right after his fall, my line of sight was blocked by an ebon-skinned two-legs. Despite my weakness, anger filled me and I snarled at the creature, flashing my own canines.

"Good! She still has fight. There may still be hope." The two-legs held his hand over me, resting it on my side.

It must have known I could not move because it moved its hands down my body without fear. I felt its probing fingers sinking into my fur as though looking for something. Too exhausted to fight, I lay my head down and endured it with whatever dignity I had left.

"I cannot find an injury," the two-legs continued, talking to someone behind me that I could not see.

"We must flip her over. It's probably on the other side." This voice was higher pitched and more soothing than the other. It came around and I got my first view of it.

I had never seen this kind of two-legs before. It had long, sun-colored hair that was pulled tightly back behind its head, almost like a lion's mane except pulled back from the face. It had eyes the color of the sky that had a tenderness much like Mother's. Its skin was very pale with spots of dull red just beneath its eyes. Other than an innate gentleness absent from the other two-legs I'd encountered, it also sported a clean, fur-free face. I think this added to its aura of gentleness. After a moment, I realized it must be the female of the species. She reached out and gently stroked my ear.

"It's going to be alright, little one," she said. Turning to her companion, she continued. "Grab her legs and gently turn her over."

I cried out in pain as they pulled on my injured leg. After successfully turning me over, I heard them both gasp.

"We have to get her to the clinic immediately," she said. "This wound is badly infected."

"What about the brother?" the male two-legs asked.

"Take his records quickly and wake him up. By the time we get her in the truck and strapped down, you need to be done."

The male nodded and left my line of sight. Other pale-skinned two-legs came up to me, one holding a strange looking thorn in its hand. It pushed it into my thigh with a sharp sting. A moment later, I fell into a sleep deeper than any I'd had since before coming to paradise.

I woke some time later feeling better than I had in days. Although I was incredibly thirsty, I felt well rested and my pain was much more manageable. I could lift my head, sit up and, most importantly, my senses had returned. I no longer felt as if I was living in a cloud. I looked around me, taking in my surroundings.

Around me were the same stone tree limbs that took me from my home. Looking out, I noticed others spaced around a strange looking cave. The walls were smooth as water with openings looking out into the plains. One of the openings caught my attention. It didn't look like the other windows. The terrain looked more like the area around the lake with the mountain far off in the distance. Also, no light showed through the opening. As I continued to look at it, I gasped in surprise. N'dugu sat in the center, looking out at the land filled with countless different animals. I called to him, trying to get his attention but he didn't even flick an ear.

The noise I made alerted the two-legs and they came in through an opening at the end of the cave. I continued to call for N'dugu to no avail. The ebon-skinned male approached my stone enclosure, a wide smile stretched across his face. His white teeth was a stark contrast to his dark skin and his midnight eyes sparkled with joy.

"I am glad you have come through!" he said. "May we check your bandages?"

His voice was friendly and soothing. For the next several minutes, he sat in front of my cage and simply talked. I had no idea what he was saying and often, he would switch to a different dialect altogether. Over time, I just lay my head down and listened to the soothing sound of his voice. Half the day had passed before he got to his feet.

"I am going to open the door, okay?" he said, reaching for the latch of my enclosure. With a soft click, the door swung open.

I looked out at the room and then up to the male. Instinct told me to run but I'd already realized that my leg would not hold my weight. In fact, there was a heavy material wrapped around it keeping it immobile. The male squatted on his heels and looked into my enclosure.

"I'm not going to take you out until you are ready, so just let me know when you are."

Several minutes later, after coming to the realization that this man meant me no harm, I scooted toward the opening. Very slowly, he approached me and reached into the cage. I allowed him to lift me and carry me to a large flat stone in the center of the cave.

"It always amazes me how easily you can gain their trust," the female said, approaching us.

"You just have to let the animals understand they have nothing to fear from you. Once you do this, you can begin to build a relationship. Animals are more intelligent than people give them credit for and they feel the same emotions as us."

"Hello, little one," she said, coming to stand in front of me. "I am Dr. Collins. This is my companion, Mustafa. We are going to get your leg fixed so that you can get back home where you belong. Your brother is very worried about you."

I cocked my head at her. While I couldn't understand her language, I understood her meaning. She was there to help me. Mustafa stroked my head, neck, and ears while Dr Collins moved around the table to my leg. Mustafa's actions were very comforting. It felt much like the same affection I shared with my brothers. Without realizing it, I closed my eyes and began purring.

Some time later, Dr. Collins finished her examination and Mustafa picked me up and carried me back to my cage. He gave me a final stroke and stood back.

"I'm going to bring you some food and then you need to get some rest. I will come back tomorrow and tell you a story if you like."

Sensing he was leaving, I chirped. I didn't really want to be alone. He chuckled, assuming I was agreeing with his storytelling idea. Closing the door, he latched it and left the room. A little later, he returned with a bowl full of meat. Right after eating it, sleep came upon me. I didn't even hear him when he removed the empty bowl from my cage.

Chapter Fifteen: Mustafa

The following weeks, I healed quickly. The wound in my leg closed and the broken bones began to mend. I could not yet walk but Mustafa often stretched out my legs, testing my flexibility. Afterward, he would sit for hours next to my cage, and later, the enclosure I was moved to. He gave me a new name, *Asha*, and said that it meant "life" in his native tongue. It was this language he spoke when it was just he and I. When the pale-skinned two-legs were around, he would speak in their language.

I found Mustafa's company soothing and his presence eased the loneliness I once felt with N'dugu's absence. His stories, though I could not understand him, were full of inflection and passion. Sometimes he would jump up and wave his hands in enthusiasm as he told a particularly interesting part of the story. If a cheetah could laugh, I would have, just because the motion was so comical. He looked like an ostrich strutting its feathers. Still, it was endearing and I gave him my full attention.

After a few weeks passed, the bandage around my leg came off and I was able to move around. The leg didn't hurt but I had limited mobility. Try as I might, I could not pull it up to my belly, nor pull it all the way back. Running down prey would be a problem if I didn't get some of the flexibility back.

Mustafa would attach a leash to the collar around my neck and walk me around the rescue center, hoping to loosen up my joints. I liked this time with him. More often than not, it was spent in companionable silence. He would reach down and scratch me behind my ears. This actually became a favorite pastime of his and he greeted me with it whenever he came to see me.

Every few days, Dr. Collins would check my progress. Sometimes she would nod her head in approval and others she would shake it, a worried expression on her face. This was something I found amazing about two-legs. They were very expressive, from their body language to their facial features to their eyes. I may not have been able to understand their speech, but their body expressions told me everything I needed to know.

One day, several weeks after coming to the rescue center, Mustafa approached me full of excitement. His addictive joy had me prancing to the enclosure door, at least as well as one can prance with a limp.

"Hello, *Asha!*" he greeted. "Today is a great day. You are going to help me teach the little ones about cheetahs."

I chirped, which was my way of agreeing to whatever it was he was saying. He clipped the leash to my collar and we headed toward the front of the rescue center. At first, a blanket of fear fell over me. I could smell the two-legs before I could see them. There were so many! It was their excitement that lifted my fear. These two-legs weren't there to hurt me. We rounded the corner and I came face to face with dozens of miniature two-legs, all wide-eyed and innocent. Mustafa led me to a small stage several feet in front of the enraptured audience.

"Hello, children!" Mustafa called. "Say hello to *Asha!*"

As one, some three dozen children said, "Hello, *Asha.*"

I did the only thing I could do; I chirped!

For the next two months, Mustafa would take me to the stage where he spoke to children, and sometimes even adults about the importance of the ecosystem, predators and prey, and where they all fit into the environment, to include "humans", a word I learned was meant for two-legs. The "humans" were always excited when I arrived, cheering when I chirped or purred. Although Mustafa often pet me, he would not let the other humans do so. For this, I was grateful. All the excitement already made me nervous. I could only imagine what it would be like to have them all trying to touch me!

One day while we were preparing to go out on stage, another human, named Francis, joined us with another cheetah. A vague sense of recognition hit me the first time I'd met Francis, as though I'd seen him before but try as I might, I couldn't figure out when that was. He spoke the same language as Dr. Collins, for the most part, but his inflection was highly accented with some other dialect, much like when I spoke with the lion.

The male cheetah he had with him was outgoing and very attentive to Francis. So much so that he barely took notice of me. I was fascinated by him because he was the only other cheetah I'd ever seen that wasn't related to me. I tried to start up a conversation but he ignored me. Not in a rude way. He just didn't seem that interested. I laid next to Mustafa and rested my head on my paws.

Mustafa, noticing my melancholy, reached down to scratch my ears. "I think Nauru has offended little *Asha*," he chuckled.

"Nauru, you should greet *Asha*. She is new here and alone," Francis said, lightly scolding the male cheetah. Nauru cocked his head and chirped. Squatting down, Francis held his hand out to me. "Come, *Asha*, and meet Nauru."

I looked up at Mustafa briefly and, with his nod, approached the pair. Nauru finally took notice of me and rose to his feet.

"Hello, Asha!" he chirped excitedly. "This is so exciting!! It's my first time going in front of the children."

"Hello, Nauru," I said. "How long have you been at the rescue center?"

"What, here?" He looked confused at first. "Oh, I don't live here. I live on a preserve away from here. Master cares for me and has been training me to talk to children. He says it will help with his mission."

"Nauru, how old are you?"

"Umm…I have not yet seen a full turn of the seasons."

"Where is your mother?"

"I don't know. I was raised by humans. Francis said something about 'poachers' but I don't know what that means."

Orphaned. I bumped my head against his in the familiar show of affection I shared with my siblings but he laughed and scuttled away, like he wanted to play. Before I could further contemplate the poor cub's circumstances, Mustafa called me and we entered the stage.

This crowd was larger than usual with both children and adults sitting in front of the stage. Francis came out after us with an overly excited Nauru. He waved his hand as he walked to Mustafa's other side.

"Hello, everyone! Today we have a special treat. Say hello to *Asha* and Nauru!" The crowd cheered and said hello. "Who can tell me how fast a cheetah can run?"

A boy in the front rose his hand but before Francis could call on him, he shouted, "Up to 75 miles per hour!"

"Oui! That is right. They run so fast their feet actually leave the ground. But this speed is hard for cheetahs to maintain and it wears them out quickly. If they are successful in bringing down prey, they may be too exhausted to eat it right away, making for easy pickings for predators. Many times, cheetahs have to abandon their kill to other predators like lions, hyenas, and sometimes, leopards.

"Because they run so fast, and they are solitary, they require large amounts of land for their territory. Unfortunately, this becomes a problem when human villages branch out into cheetah lands. Humans and cheetahs clash over land and food and often, cheetahs are killed as nuisance animals. Today, there are less than 10,000 wild cheetahs left in the world."

Francis continued to talk to the other humans for some time. Occasionally, they would gasp or clap, depending on what he said. Once, they all burst out laughing. When Francis was finished, Mustafa came out and told my story. After that, the show ended and we made our way backstage. Mustafa told Francis and Nauru good-bye and turned to leave.

"Good-bye, Nauru," I called over my shoulder.

"Bye, Asha," he said, barely sparing me a glance.

The summer ended and the rainy season began. For the first time since coming to the rescue center, I was overcome with a feeling of loss. I missed my brother but this feeling went deeper than that. It didn't take long to realize what it was. Every year I bore witness to the renewal of the land. I lavished in the green sprouts and tiny, colorful flowers, the new life beginning all around me. I missed all of that while stuck behind the cages of the rescue center. The worst part came with the knowledge that, even though my leg was healed, I still could not return to my home.

One morning, when I was especially depressed, I heard Mustafa and Dr. Collins speaking in heated voices. They were walking toward my enclosure and Mustafa's hands were waving as they did when he became excited or agitated.

"She must be moved, Mustafa. There isn't enough room to keep her here and she can't return to the wild," she said, holding her hands up in defense.

"She doesn't belong in a zoo! If you give me time, I can get her leg back to where it needs to be."

"She's had three months. She should already be walking fine. I think a lot of it is mental." Dr. Collins stopped and pinched the bridge of her nose. In a softer voice, probably too soft for Mustafa to hear, she said, "What good would it do? Her habitat is shrinking. There just isn't enough room for cheetahs and people in Africa anymore."

The tension in the room alarmed me and I chirped my discomfort. Mustafa turned to me, a look of profound sadness clouding his eyes.

Looking back to Dr. Collins, he said, "She will waste away in a zoo so far from her home. She needs to run." He turned and approached my enclosure. In his native tongue, he said, "I am sorry, *Asha*. It was my duty to protect you and I failed."

He reached through the bars and scratched me behind my ears. I closed my eyes and butted my head against his hand, rubbing my scent into his dark skin. A rumbling purr issued from my chest and

Mustafa chuckled. I feared this would be the last time I ever saw him. When he pulled his hand away, I opened my eyes and looked up. His onyx orbs swam with moisture but before any tears could fall, he got to his feet and stormed from the room.

Dr. Collins looked from the door and back to me, a look of helplessness marring her features. "He is right but my hands are tied. I am so sorry, little one."

Chapter Sixteen: Forsaken

The next few days were filled with a flurry of activity. Mustafa did not come to see me and I missed his company and his walks. A few hours before I was set to leave, I lay curled up in a transport carrier in the rescue center. Despite all the preparations outside, it was quiet where I was. I faced away from the door, contemplating everything that had happened since leaving my home, all that I had lost and gained. All that I had learned.

It surprised me to learn that there were good two-legs, and not just the bad ones Mother and M'vita had warned me about. I suppose it made sense. After all, there were some animals that were more hostile than others. I remembered a story Mother once told me about a baboon that fought fiercely over a scrap of food. Its large canines scared off a young lion who ran back to its pride whimpering like a cub, even though it was already half grown.

As I sank deeper into my memories, my mind drifted to N'dugu. I worried for my brother. How was he getting along without me? Without even knowing that I still lived? Had he found any other cheetahs in my absence? My biggest fear and greatest hope was that he left Paradise altogether to search for cheetahs elsewhere. If he could not fulfill the prophesy in Paradise, he needed to leave and go where he was most needed.

Of course, if he did, and I ever managed to find my way back there, I would never see him again. I sighed deeply. The chances were grim I'd ever see either of my homes again. If the humans had their way, and if my leg never healed, I would spend the rest of my life in a cage. Curling tighter in my ball, I tried to remember my youngest days, when everything was safe and perfect. So lost in my memories, I didn't even hear the door open or the person approaching my cage until they spoke.

"Hello, *Asha*," Mustafa called softly. I jumped in surprise and turned to see him sitting on the floor next to my cage. "I am sorry I did not come see you sooner. Did you miss me?"

I rubbed my head and shoulders against the bars and purred. Mustafa chuckled, pushing his fingers through the bars in an attempt to scratch my head. Sighing, he pulled his hand free and turned around, leaning his back against the bars. Sensing his sadness and frustration, I laid down on the other side, pushing, as best I could, against his back. I slipped a paw out and rested it on his arm. He sucked in a deep breath and lowered his head, placing his hand over my paw.

I chirped to get his attention. Something was very wrong. The emotions rolling off his shoulders were destructive and I wanted to distract him from them. He turned to look at me, trails of moisture slipping down his face.

"I'm really going to miss you," he said. "I hope that one day, I will be able to see you again. How about one more story while we wait? This is a story about a brave little cheetah who was taken from her home to a new land full of danger where she is injured and taken away. And just when all seems lost, she finds her way back home."

I listened for the next couple of hours as Mustafa told his tale. Then, Dr. Collins and Francis came in to take me away. Mustafa waved until I could no longer see him. Just before loading the conveyance that would take me to my new home, Francis approached me. He carefully stretched out his hand to scratch my head. Even though he wasn't Mustafa, I allowed it because I trusted him.

"Do not worry, *Asha*," he said. "I am coming with you so you will not be alone."

I chirped, understanding the meaning, if not the words of what he said. He smiled and rubbed me again. Then, Dr.Collins pushed a thorn into my hip and a cool liquid filled my body. A few moments later, sleep found me.

I remember nothing of the trip to my new home, as I slept the whole way. I woke with a mighty thirst and stiff joints. By the time I opened my eyes, I was already out of my cage and laying on another flat stone in the middle of a very white room. Francis stood nearby and came when he realized I was awake.

"Hello, *Asha*," he said, placing a bowl of water in front of me. "How are you feeling? Are you ready to meet your new companions?"

I didn't mean to ignore him but I was so thirsty. When the bowl was empty, he took it away and clipped a leash to my collar.

"Are you ready to take her out?" a tall female said behind him.

"Yes, but I am worried about how she will handle it. She has nev'r really been in close contact with other cheetahs except for her siblings."

"She will do fine. The others are used to being housed together. They will except her as one of their own."

Francis nodded and followed her, pulling me along with him. We traveled through a land of cages. Some of the animals I'd seen before but there were many more that were foreign to me. And every one of them were trapped. After some time, we reached the cheetah enclosure. The walk had been long but my stiff joints needed it. Now, I wanted to run away. The female led the way into the enclosure and Francis coaxed me into following him.

The space was much larger than my enclosure at the rescue center but not large enough for me to run. How was I supposed to get my strength back if I couldn't run? In a sheltered corner near the back, I could see three other cheetah lounging. That was when I realize two other things. First, there was no rain. It should still be the rainy season but not a drop fell from the crystal clear sky. Second, it was cold, colder than I'd ever felt in all my life. I stopped in my tracks and looked up at Francis, chirping my discomfort.

Francis lowered himself down to look me in the eyes and rubbed me behind my ears. "I know it isn't ideal," he said. "But it is just for a little while, until you get your strength back. Then, I will take you back home. I promise."

With those words, he unclipped my collar and stood back. As I was looking at the far corner, and the suddenly interested cheetahs, Francis and the female slipped out. I heard the latch close and turned around to see I was alone. When I turned back, the three cheetahs were walking toward me.

"Look what we have here," one of them said. She was the only female. "You look scared as a kitten. Come get warm with us."

"Okay," I said, not denying her observation.

"My name is Shiba," she said. "This here is Maddox and Vince. What's your name, sweetheart?"

"I'm Sahara." Shiba walked next to me with Maddox close to her side. Vince walked a bit further behind and scanned around as if looking for danger. "Are you siblings?"

Shiba scoffed and threw a look at Maddox. "Vince and I are. But...we *were* all born here. What is your story?"

"I was born out there," I said, looking out past the enclosure. "Three of my brothers and I were taken from our home and moved somewhere else, an unfamiliar land. But, we lost Kana soon after arriving and Soji was killed by hunters. I was attacked by a rogue lion and brought to the rescue center. I can't run yet, so they brought me here. I need to get back to my brother, N'dugu. He is prophesied to save the cheetahs."

At first, they just stood there and stared at me. It made me slightly uncomfortable until Vince took a step toward me.

"You survived all of that?" he asked, amazement filling his voice.

"Yes, because of my brothers. Without them, I would not have."

"Wow!" Shiba said. "That's amazing. I've never heard of a prophesy before. Why do the cheetahs need saving?"

Now it was my turn to stand amazed. "You really don't know?" They all shook their heads. "The cheetahs are disappearing in the wild. If something doesn't happen, there will be none left. As it is, N'dugu and I are the only ones in Paradise."

Shiba and Maddox shook their heads and turned back to the shelter, deep in a conversation only they could hear. Vince came up beside me, a silent comfort I didn't even realize I needed. Together, we walked the rest of the way to the shelter. Once there, he offered me a spot near his pallet to sleep off my exhaustion. I was grateful for him and the others. Meeting new cheetahs was both exciting and scary.

Shiba, Maddox, and Vince were all younger than me, although Vince was slightly older than the other two, born a turn of the seasons before. Their age and inexperience created a barrier between us that I hoped I would be able to break down. That night was the first of many where homesickness would keep me from a restful slumber.

Chapter Seventeen: Solitude

The next few days passed in boredom, at least for me. With nothing to do all day, I chafed at the desire to run, or hunt, anything other than sitting around doing nothing. The others seemed perfectly content to laze the day away. Occasionally, a group of two-legs would walk past the enclosure. I would approach them, hoping for a chance to relive some of the excitement from the rescue center. But these two-legs not only looked different, they didn't really seem all that excited to see me. This left me with a hollow feeling in the pit of my stomach.

I spent the day walking the border of the enclosure. One reason was so that I could rebuild my strength. If I ever wanted to run again, I'd have to have the strength and mobility. The second reason was to stay warm. The chill in the air was strange after leaving the heat of an African dry season.

I think my pacing annoyed Shiba because she began to keep her distance from me. Not only that, she urged the same of Maddox and Vince, although it seemed to pain the latter. I didn't care. I was on a mission and these captive-bred cheetah couldn't help me. I ignored her scalding looks and went on with my day.

Feeding time came once a day and it didn't take long for me to figure out where I stood in the pecking order. I didn't like being fed. I was a hunter and I wanted to hunt. However, my choices were grim. I could either eat the strange meat they fed me or I could go hungry. The others didn't seem to mind and crowded the entrance to claim their food. Being last, I was left with the least desirable portions.

At first, Francis came with the food to check on me. I ached for his presence because it was the only thing that was familiar. He would show me some affection and speak to me for several minutes, always promising me he'd find some way to get me home. Then he would once again leave me to my solitude. I think his visits further isolated me from Shiba and the others. They did not allow the two-legs to touch them. Because I did so, among everything else that made me different, Shiba did not see me as a cheetah at all. She would openly snub me and would not allow me to sleep near them. In fact, I couldn't even get close to the shelter without her flashing her teeth at me.

So, I kept my distance. I found a spot on the farthest part of the enclosure where a large rock sat. It was a perfect spot for sunning and getting lost in my contemplations. It was one of these times I'd taken notice of my nearest neighbor. Normally, I wouldn't have paid more than a moment's notice to those around me but this creature had me both confused and curious.

It looked like nature had gotten something wrong, as though it were putting together a jigsaw puzzle but instead of putting the pieces in the right order, it had just given up and glued them in some haphazard way. It had small horns on its head, like the budding horns of a young antelope, except that they were covered in fur. Its face was long and narrow, like a giraffe, but its eyes were smaller and snout rounded. It had large ears and a long neck like an antelope.

While its back sloped slightly, it was not nearly as pronounced as that of a giraffe and its body was heavy and muscled like that of a horse. Its legs were also strong and stout, like a horse. Its tail, however, was anything but equine. It was similar to a giraffe with a small tuft of fur at the end. Stranger still, was the coloration of the animal. Most of its body was covered in a rich mahogany that shimmered in the sunlight. However, its legs and rump were covered in white stripes, like that of a zebra. While its legs resembled those of a horse, or a zebra, its feet were cloven and looked almost too small to support the animal's weight.

As a young one approached the barrier between our enclosures, it lifted its head, sticking out its long tongue to reach the leaves of the tree in my enclosure. I stared, amazed and unable to look away. Eventually, my blatant stares were noticed. The young animal looked down at me, chewing a mouthful of leaves.

"Hello," it said around its lunch.

"Hello," I answered, not wanting to be rude.

"You must be new. I've never seen you before."

"I just arrived a few moons ago."

"I'm Nala. What's your name?" he said, swallowing the leaves.

"Sahara. I don't mean to be rude but my curiosity is killing me. What are you?"

Nala chuckled. "Curiosity killed the cat." Noticing that I didn't get the joke, he continued. "I'm an Okapi."

"A what?" I asked, cocking my head to the side.

"An Okapi. My mom says we live deep in the forest where the sun rarely reaches the ground. I can't imagine never seeing the sun! Mom also says it's too quite here. She said, in the forest, there is always noise: monkeys, birds, and leopards. The forest is so dense, you never even see the animals. Even at night, the forest is alive with music. She has a hard time sleeping because it is so quite."

"Have you never seen your home?"

"No. I was born here. Mom says we will probably never go home. I think it makes her sad."

"Why can't you go home?"

"Mom says there isn't enough room. She was brought here because the two-legs cut down the trees in her forest. She had nowhere else to go."

"I can't go home, either," I said, looking down at my leg stretched out next to me.

"Why? Is your home disappearing, too?"

"Yes. There is not enough room and too many two-legs. The lions have also taken control of what little land remains. They kill anything that poses a threat. It isn't their fault, really. It's just a need for survival."

"Is that what happened to your leg?"

"I was too hungry to give up my meal without a fight. If it wasn't for my brother, I probably wouldn't have gotten away."

"Well, it's nice here. Plenty of food and it's safe. I think you will like it."

"Thanks," I said, but I didn't feel grateful. That kind of outlook could only be seen by someone who had never been free.

Nala's mom called him away and, with a farewell shake of his head, he ambled over to her.

I watched them for a while later. Something familiar tingled the back of my mind, like maybe I had seen one of them before. After a while, I curled up on my rock and closed my eyes.

The following weeks were much the same. My exercise paid off and I could feel my leg loosening and stretching more. I wasn't a hundred percent sure I could take down an impala but I would give it a run for its money. The tension between Shiba and I grew worse and what was once annoyance at my presence had become hostility. She considered the enclosure her territory and I had intruded upon it with my strange ways and free spirit.

During meals, after the two-legs left, she would lunge for me, sometimes taking my meal in the process. I didn't always escape unscathed and began to sport injuries on my head, neck, and sometimes, my back. Maddox stood by, probably afraid of raising her ire. After one particularly brutal encounter where she actually had me pinned to the ground, I decided to stay far away from her. I couldn't really blame her. I would be protective of my territory as well.

With a sore jaw and an empty stomach, I limped over to my rock. It was a long and slow walk but I didn't mind. Just a bit longer and I could go home. I settled myself on the rock and looked out at the world beyond my walls.

"She doesn't really mean anything, you know," Vince said behind me.

I brought my head around to look at him. It was the first any of them had talked to me in weeks. At his feet sat his untouched meal. My stomach growled but I turned back around, facing away from him.

"I know," I said.

"I'm sorry for how we are treating you. I know it can't be easy for you, losing everything you've ever known and then having to live somewhere you don't feel wanted."

I didn't say anything but my stomach twisted at his words. I missed my brother and our new home desperately. The tearing sensation of loss in my chest never went away, especially when I thought of everything I was missing out on.

"I want to be your friend, Sahara."

At this, I sat up and turned to face him. "What about Shiba? I don't think she would like you spending time with me."

"Shiba can take care of herself. And she has Maddox. Let me take care of you." He reached down and picked up his food. Slowly, he walked up to me and placed it on my rock.

I wanted his friendship so I accepted his offering. After I finished, he smiled, as only a cheetah can and bumped his head against mine, following it with a long rub down my cheek and neck. I almost cried at the form of endearment. I hadn't felt that since the last time I was with N'dugu. Sensing my sadness, Vince curled up next to me and I leaned against his side.

For the next week, Vince and I spent all our time together. We ran the perimeter, climbed rocks, chased down the occasional rodent that scurried through the enclosure. He was actually pretty fit for a captive-bred and raised cheetah. In many ways, he reminded me of Soji. When we weren't exercising, I would tell him stories of my homes, especially Paradise and its unimaginable beauty. Of course, this got me thinking about Mustafa and his stories and I would tell Vince about him as well.

Throughout this time, Vince and I formed a bond as strong as my brothers and I. I could no longer imagine being without him. He became my comfort and solace. But this new bond shattered any chance of acceptance from Shiba.

Chapter Eighteen: Out of Time

Even being as far from home as I was, surrounded
by near freezing temperatures, I knew deep down
that the rainy season was coming to an end in
Paradise. My heart ached for a chance to see the
world come back to life, especially after everything
that I had gone through. I must have whimpered in
my sleep because Vince rested his chin across my

back in an effort to sooth me. Grateful for his company and warmth, I curled up closer to him.

"Is everything alright?" he asked, his breath tickling my ear.

"I'm just thinking about home," I answered and sighed.

"You will get back there. But, for now, let's go fetch breakfast!"

We got to our feet, shook out our coats, and made our way to the entrance for food. Shiba and Maddox had yet to arrive and I hoped we would miss them altogether. Unfortunately, I had no such luck.

"Vince, how could you," she said, accusingly. "She isn't even one of us."

Vince, for his part, tried to ignore her and placed himself between me and her. Maddox, as usual, stood off to the side, a silent observer.

"Shiba, I don't want to fight-" I started.

I never finished what I wanted to say. The she-cat plowed through the unsuspecting Vince and rammed me into the ground. All my instincts kicked in and, for a moment, I thought I was fighting the lion once again. I'm not really sure what happened next. All I can remember is the snarling, biting, and clawing. One minute she was above me, snapping at my face and the next, I was being pulled off of her by the two-legs. Shiba lay whimpering on the ground. Vince squared off with the two-legs holding my collar, his body low and a growl emanating from his throat. That was when another two-legs came in and pushed a thorn into my thigh. I watched Vince being hauled away as my vision slowly faded and I was lost to the world of dreams.

When I awoke, I was in a tiny cage surrounded by other tiny cages. I had just enough room to stand and turn around. The room was neither dark nor bright but somewhere in between with lots of shadows. And it was utterly quiet. I chirped loudly to try and get someone's attention. *What am I doing here?* I'd been separated from the other cheetah. It wasn't my fault. I was just defending myself.

A long time later, the door at the end of the room finally opened. Francis entered with another two-legs I'd never seen before. They were talking just outside of my enclosure, their stressed voices arguing back and forth.

"We don't have a choice. We have to euthanize her," said the unfamiliar two-legs, a male wearing a long white coat.

"Non! I do not accept that. Can we not move her to another facility?" Francis urged.

"She's lame, and wild. She'll have the same problem no matter where we send her. I'm sorry, but this is the only way. It's humane and the best thing for her."

"I promised I would look out for her. I cannot let this happen."

"Look, I understand what you are saying but she attacked another cheetah. She's territorial and, really, she was too old to be taken from the wild. She's not going to change and the next time, she may kill another animal, or even a human. Can you, in good conscience, allow that to happen?"

Francis stood there, helpless.

"Tomorrow morning, doctor," the two-legs in the white coat continued. "I suggest you say your goodbyes." With that, he left, leaving Francis and me alone in the room.

Francis sat down next to my cage and stared at me. The scene was eerily familiar to the last time I'd seen Mustafa and I wondered if I was going to yet another home, temporary or not. But Francis' expression was even more dire than Mustafa's had been.

"*Je suis désolé*. I promised Mustafa I would take care of you," he said. At the mention of Mustafa, I stood up and chirped. He chuckled sadly and placed his hand on the metal of the cage. "What am I supposed to do now?"

I rubbed my body as best I could against the metal where his hand was and purred deeply. I wanted to feel his fingers scratch me behind the ears. He didn't move, however, leaving his hand where it was.

"I do not believe you attacked that other cheetah," he said. "Look at you. You are like a *chaton*. How could anyone think you are violent?"

Realizing he wasn't going to pet me, I curled up in a ball and looked up at him. Moisture swam in his eyes and ran down his cheeks. This overwhelming emotion flowed from him to me and all I wanted to do was remove it from him. Perhaps it was the look in my eyes, or his promise to his friend, but at that moment, he'd made a life-changing decision.

"I am going to take you out of here and get you back home where you belong. I would rather you take your chances in the wild than to die in here without a fight."

With that, he stood up and marched from the room.

Late that night, Francis came quietly into the room, opened up my cage, and clipped a leash to my collar.

Without saying a word, we slipped from the building. The zoo was quiet with most of the lights turned off or muted. The cloudy sky offered nothing in the way of light and I wondered how Francis found his way in the darkness.

We traveled for quite a way before I realized we were leaving the zoo. The cheetah enclosure was near. All of a sudden, I thought about Vince. Vince! I couldn't leave him! I pulled at my leash, causing Francis to stumble in the dark.

"*Asha*," he whispered. "We need to leave. Come now!"

I chirped softly, finally making it to the enclosure. Francis tugged lightly on the leash. Vince must have stayed near the entrance because he came up to me a moment later.

"Sahara," he sighed. "Are you alright?"

"Yes, but..." my throat clogged with emotion. "I have to leave. I'm going back home."

"What?" I could sense Vince's despair but I could do nothing to alleviate it.

"I'm going to miss you, Vince. You made me feel almost like I was home again."

Francis reached for my collar to give me a firmer tug.

"Sahara, wait!" Vince called, following us along the enclosure. "Please don't go!"

With a final tug, Francis pulled me away from the enclosure and Vince. Once again, I felt a sense of loss so profound, I stumbled in my run.

"I am sorry we had to leave him, *Asha*. I cannot take both of you away safely. Maybe, someday, I can reunite him with you."

I followed along silently. His words were meant to soothe but all I could think about was that I was once again alone.

Chapter Nineteen: Paradise

After slipping quietly out of the zoo gates, Francis led me along a stone road where several human conveyances sat. The back of one lifted up, revealing a dark maw concealing a cage similar to the one I'd just left. I hesitated and Francis scratched me behind my ear.

"It is alright, *ma petite*," he reassured. "It will be safer for you in there and more comfortable. You trust me, yes?"

I looked into his eyes and found no reason to fear him. With a soft chirp, I took a step toward the cage. Francis helped me climb into the cage and I curled into a ball. A moment later, he opened the door in front of the conveyance and the creature came to life, purring softly beneath my cage.

The ride was a long one and I drifted in and out of sleep. The next time we stopped, the sun was cresting the horizon. Francis opened my cage and offered me some water. While I was drinking, he pushed a thorn into my hip. Truthfully, the thorns were really starting to get on my nerves. Not long after, I was drifting off to sleep. The last thing I remember was a dark-skinned two-legs approaching us.

When I once again opened my eyes, the first thing I registered was the warmth that had been absent from me for so long. My eyes were blurry and my body felt groggy. With my senses dampened, I had a moment where I entertained the idea that I was still a cub, experiencing the world for the first time: my first spring where everything was pure and new.

It only lasted a moment, however. Soon, I heard voices and realized I wasn't alone, and I wasn't safe and sound in my childhood burrow with my mother and all my siblings.

"Good morning, *ma petite*," Francis said next to me. He ran his fingers softly down my side in a soothing nature. "Are you ready to go back home?"

He tested my bad leg, pushing and pulling it to see if it caused me any pain and to ensure it had flexibility. Apparently satisfied, he smiled and released me.

"I have given you a new radio collar so that we can keep track of you. If not for the last one, the lion may have finished you off. Be careful out there, *bien*?"

I sat up and bumped my head against his. He chuckled sadly and wrapped his arms around me.

"I am really going to miss you, *ma petite.*"

Reaching under me, he lifted me and set me on the ground. He clipped a leash to my collar and led me around the conveyance. I stopped in my tracks when I realized where I was. Paradise stretched before me in all its spring glory. Some ways off, I could see the lake and the countless herds meandering through the green grasses. Flocks of birds flew this way and that, filling the sky with color and movement. At the farthest end of my field of vision, on the very edge of the horizon, was the peak of the mountain I'd seen while Soji still lived.

I looked up at Francis, torn between staying with him and returning home. My whole body ached to stretch my legs and just run. Was N'dugu still in Paradise or did he leave?

"Come, *Asha.* Let us go for a walk," Francis said, moving away from his conveyance.

We were maybe half-way to the lake when he stopped again. He took several minutes and just observed everything around him. I could see and feel the wonder in him. I knew that feeling. It was the same thing I felt every spring. With a sigh, he reached down and unclipped my collar.

"Go, *ma petite*. You are home."

My desire for freedom outweighed anything else I felt. With one final rub against his leg, I opened my legs and ran. It felt so good to run! A few moments later, I turned back, concerned for my friend. Francis stood on top of a hill looking down at me. He was not alone. I suddenly realized Mustafa stood next to him.

With a wave, Francis called, "*Au revoir, Asha! May we meet again some day.*"

For one moment, I considered going back. Then, I heard a familiar chirp. N'dugu! My brother had caught sight of me and was calling from some ways off. I turned from my two-legged friends and ran to find my brother.

~Three months later~

Life had returned to normal over the months of my return. The lions had settled and were no longer a problem for me. At least no more than usual. N'dugu told me the old male that had attacked me had died not long after I left, probably from wounds or starvation. Other two-legs now patrolled the territory, protecting the wildlife from hunters. They did not interact with anyone other than each other and N'dugu had gained a grudging respect for them.

Life had continued on without me. Except for one thing. There were still no cheetah in Paradise, save N'dugu and now me. He confessed that he almost left. So deep was his despair and loneliness, he nearly left Paradise altogether in the hopes of finding others like us. I ached for him. But, I also had pains of my own.

I told N'dugu about everything that happened to me. All the creatures that I had met and the adventures that I had. Lastly, I told him of Vince and how I wished he could have come back with me.

Shortly after my return, N'dugu left for his own home. Knowing that I was home and safe was enough for him to be content and we returned to our lives of solitude. Of course, we were never really alone.

Despite my heartbreak over Vince, he left me with the most precious gift anyone could give. Nearly three months after returning home, I was blessed with a litter of my own, four beautiful cubs that shared traits with both me and Vince. It was three little girls and one boy. A new generation of cheetah. A new start for a species once gone from Paradise.

Save the Cheetah
Save the Planet

Conservation Efforts

In the early 1900's, more than 100,000 cheetah existed throughout Africa and Asia to include five different subspecies. Preferring steppes, savannah, grasslands, and acacia scrubs, they once roamed these habitats from the Cape Peninsula all the way to the Mediterranean and the Arabian Peninsula to India. After half a century of sport hunting, their numbers drastically decreased, becoming extinct in some areas, such as Arabia and India. Today, cheetahs have been eradicated from thirteen countries where they once lived, primarily by farmers believing the cheetah were a threat to their flocks and trophy hunters. Another threat to wild cheetahs is the illegal pet trade, where cheetah cubs are taken from the wild and sold as pets. As of today, there are around 10,000 cheetahs left in the wild with a population of around 50 Asiatic cheetahs in Iran.

One of the biggest natural threats to cheetahs is cub mortality, most often by other predators such as lions, hyenas, and leopards and can be as high as 90% in some areas. With shrinking habitats, this brings predators closer together and raises this number.

Asiatic Cheetahs

Once ranging across the Arabian Peninsula to India, through Iran, Central Asia, Afghanistan, and Pakistan, this once flourishing subspecies of cheetah today is critically endangered with around 50 individuals existing only in Iran (Mallon). They are extinct throughout the rest of their natural range.

Asiatic cheetahs are generally smaller than their African cousins and exist primarily in dry desert environments. In the harsh Iranian winters, these cheetahs develop a thicker coat, especially around the neck and upper back. Today, most live in wildlife sanctuaries. 40% of Asiatic cheetah deaths are due to collisions with traffic. In an effort to raise awareness for these highly endangered animals, the Iranian national football team used the cheetah's symbol on their jerseys for the 2014 FIFA World Cup ("FIFA...").

India is currently attempting to reintroduce the Asiatic cheetah back into the country.

King Cheetah

This story highlights a unique mutation of some African cheetahs, similar to a black jaguar or white lion. Despite the belief that the king cheetah was a subspecies of cheetah, it has been shown that the unique splotchy pattern, as described on N'dugu, is actually a mutation of a regular African cheetah. Because the gene is recessive, it does not always pass from parent to offspring. Unfortunately, this unique mutation makes the king cheetah a prime target for trophy hunters.

What's Being Done

Many programs worldwide are working to raise awareness and educate people on the importance of cheetahs in the wild and our part in it. The biggest threats against cheetahs are human settlements that border cheetah lands. Farmers, fearing the cheetahs will hunt their livestock, kill the large cats, despite the fact that cheetahs do not eat livestock if they have any other choice. They prefer the hunt. Conservation groups are working with local villages to educate them and setting them up with anti-predator options, such as dogs, which cheetahs will not approach.

Another thing being done on the local level is the hiring of locals to deter poachers. Many animals are killed for food by poor villages. By hiring these people to protect the animals, it gives villages the opportunity to feed their families without having to hunt endangered and threatened species.

Lastly, there are countless conservation groups working to ensure the survival of the cheetah and other vulnerable species and habitats in Africa. These include groups like WCS (Wildlife Conservation Society), Cheetah Preservation Foundation, the Cheetah Conservation Fund, the Okapi Conservation Project, and Gorongosa National Park among many, many others.

Cheetah Conservation Fund

http://cheetah.org/

In 1990, Dr Laurie Marker founded what would become one of the largest cheetah conservation projects in the world, with branches in different countries all with the purpose of preserving this magnificent species. She works with locals and other countries to develop successful predator-friendly livestock management. By studying cheetahs both in the wild and in captivity, CCF staff use their research to educate countries on how to best preserve the cheetahs and the human-predator relationships.

"CCF's conservation programming is rooted in scientific research. CCF maintains a research program on the biology, ecology and genetics of cheetahs that publishes papers in peer-reviewed journals annually, and currently operates the only fully-equipped genetics lab at an in-situ conservation facility in Africa.

Using this research as an underpinning, CCF has created a set of integrated programs that together address the threats both to the cheetah and its entire ecosystem, including human populations. CCF operates from the principle that only by securing the future of the communities that live alongside the cheetah can you secure a future for the cheetah. Helping people helps cheetahs." ("What We Do")

Fossil Rim Wildlife Center

http://fossilrim.org/

Located in Glen Rose, Texas, Fossil Rim may seem like the last place to find cheetahs. However, this wildlife preserve in the Middle of Texas works diligently to educate people a half a world away from their native habitat. Cheetahs are also notoriously difficult to breed in captivity. Fossil Rim has seen the birth of 100 cubs since 1986.

"Fossil Rim was founded on the conviction that all creatures have a right to exist; that the natural world has intrinsic value apart from human perceptions and needs; and that this right and this value deserve our deep respect.

Modern culture, with its emphasis on economic and technological values, tends to threaten the quality and integrity of nature.

Fossil Rim strives to provide a model and stimulus for alternative ways of experiencing and relating to animals and nature as a whole." ("Our Philosophy")

Gorongosa National Park

http://www.gorongosa.org

Most of my research comes from the countless documentaries I'd watched from childhood through today. Like most children, I was fascinated by the fastest land animal and again, like most children, my heart broke when they, and other African animals began to disappear, many caught up in the human wars that spread across the countries. However, my desire to write about their plight came after watching a particularly heartbreaking documentary that wasn't even really about them. In fact, the cheetahs have been completely eradicated from this part of Africa.

The documentary was titled, "Africa's Lost Eden." It is a story of Gorongosa National Park in Mozambique and how a once thriving nature preserve with the most diverse ecosystem in all of Africa was nearly erased from existence. In fact, during a decades long civil war, 95% of the animals in the park disappeared, including the cheetahs. Over the last several years, efforts have been made to boost the ecosystem, strengthening animal populations that are already there and bringing in animals when needed, such as elephants and hippos.

In 2011, GNP attempted to reintroduce three cheetahs back into the park. Unfortunately, two were killed by poachers and the third by an antelope. For now, they have decided to hold off reintroducing any more until they can assure their safety.

While I based a lot of my information off of Gorongosa's story, I did not use the park directly. I purposely left out any definitive area for this story. That being said, it is my greatest hope that cheetahs return to this beautiful oasis that I have aptly named "paradise" in my book.

What You Can Do

The greatest weapon against extinction is education. Read this book and others like it. Study the websites I have listed here and many of the others that can be found across the web. Start support groups to raise funds and awareness. You would be surprised how loud a voice can be when added to many. Get involved in any way that you can. The Cheetah Conservation Fund is an excellent place to do this. Not only is it full of educational materials, there are many ways in which you can help cheetahs right from your home.

This book and all the others in the Nature's Guardians series help these conservation groups by reaching readers. Also, a portion of the proceeds from the sale of the book and collection sets go directly to conservation efforts.

Additional Resources:

Wildlife Conservation Society

http://www.wcs.org

"WCS is committed to protecting the world's wildlife. We have a bold vision for the future and a strategic plan to lead the way."

Cheetah Preservation Foundation

http://www.cango.co.za/CPF.php

"The Cheetah Preservation Foundation was founded in 1988, with the principal aim of ensuring the survival of the cheetah and other endangered species, as well as educating our visitors about the plight of the these animals. The Cheetah Preservation Foundation also gives our visitors the opportunity to become pro-active in the conservation of endangered species, by joining as members and thereby contributing financially to our various conservation projects."

Okapi Conservation Project

http://www.okapiconservation.org

"Okapi Conservation Project (OCP) works in the heart of the Democratic Republic of Congo to protect the natural habitat of the endangered okapi and indigenous Mbuti pygmies living in the Okapi Wildlife Reserve. Designated as a World Heritage Site, the Reserve is one of the most biologically diverse areas in all of Africa. Its model programs in sustainability and stewardship promote the viability of the region's biodiversity and survival of native species like the okapi, which is under increasing threat from habitat destruction and illegal human activities.

OCP focuses on developing an economic and educational foundation on which the Okapi Wildlife Reserve can operate.

This is achieved through programs in wildlife protection, alternative agriculture, and community assistance, and by working with the Institute in Congo for the Conservation of Nature (ICCN), a government organization responsible for the protection of the Reserve. Support for OCP activities comes from a global network of zoos, conservation funds, and private donors."

Resources:

Mallon, D. P. (2007). "Cheetahs in Central Asia: A historical summary" (PDF). *Cat News 46: 4–7.*

"FIFA chief green-lights Iranian cheetah logo for Iran team jersey". Tehran Times. 9 November 2013.

"What We Do". *cheetah.org.* Cheetah Conservation Fund. Web. 20 November 2015. Retrieved from http://cheetah.org/what-we-do/

"Our Philosophy". *Fossil Rim.* Web. 20 November 2015. Retrieved from http://www.fossilrim.org/conservation.php

http://www.gorongosa.org

"Africa's Lost Eden." http://www.imdb.com/title/tt1612227/

M'vita's Struggle
Nature's Guardians Series Book 4
(excerpt)

Chapter One: Family

The world I was born into can only be described as saturated with energy. It was early spring in Africa, a time of rebirth and warmth. The seasonal rains had passed and the world was bright and green. Even before I could see or hear, I could smell the land growing around me. It wasn't long before my blurry eyes opened to a world that would become my own.

I had ten siblings that Mother, Father, and the rest of the pack doted over. Our pack was large. So large, in fact, I lost count of how many individuals actually lived among us. And every one of them emitted their own energy. I can't ever remember a quiet moment in those early days, except for when the pack slept.

In the early days, when my legs refused to work properly, Mother kept us ensconced in her burrow, hidden from the countless predators prowling through the grasses. It wasn't long, however, that we outgrew our tiny home and began to venture outside into the warm daylight. I loved these excursions the most. The beauty of the world around me tempted me too much to stay hidden.

The best thing about having such a large family is the limitless food. It seemed like every member had a morsel to share with us after a hunt. Our bellies were always full and we were surrounded by boundless love and affection. Oh yeah, and we always had a baby sitter when the rest of the pack left to hunt. Sometimes, the guardian was not much older than us.

One particular afternoon, a few weeks after we began venturing out of the burrow, my oldest brother had the bright idea of slipping past the young guardian. She faced away from us and lay still so long, we believed she was sleeping. Still, I had a tiny thread of doubt eating away at me.

"Sasha," I whispered in by brother's over-large ear. "I don't think this is a good idea."

His satellite ear flicked back, smacking me in the nose. "It's fine, M'vita. She'll never know we're gone."

Despite my better judgement, I followed Sasha and my other nine siblings from the shelter of the burrow. We had just made it to the edge of the clearing when we felt a warm breeze against our necks. As one, we turned to the irate face of our guardian.

Standing tall above us, she smiled mischievously and cocked her head. "Now, where could you little demons be slipping off to?" she asked with mock sweetness.

"Just getting some fresh air," Sasha answered, his shoulders hunched under the weight of her stare.

Her smile disappeared and she pulled back her lips, flashing her canines. It was all the warning we needed. We ran back to the burrow, our white-tufted tails tucked between our legs!

Also Available:

The *Haji's Fight for Freedom* collector set includes an autographed copy of the book, a collectable falcon from Wild Republic w/ authentic bird calls, and an adoption certificate.

Follow Haji in this coming of age story about a young falcon trying to find his way in the world. Facing the death of his father at the hands of humans and then abandoned by his mother, Haji's only solace lies in the companionship of his brother, Koru. But when Koru leaves with his life-mate, Haji finds himself alone. Soon after, the same humans who killed his father, return. Find out what happens when Haji is shot from the sky!

Collection can be purchased on the Nature's Guardians website: http://www.naturesguardiansbookseries.com

The *Timber's Gambit* collection set includes an autographed copy of the book, an 8" collectable plush (through Wild Republic), and an adoption certificate. It can also be purchased through the Nature's Guardian website (listed above).

Young Timber is a grey wolf born into the largest pack in North America. Growing up as son to the great alpha, Zeus, he has the respect of the entire pack. However, after he causes a much needed hunt to fail, Zeus convinces him to find a pack of his own. Facing mountain lions, rival wolf packs, and humans, Timber treks out across the wilderness in search of the companionship and protection of a pack of his own. What will Timber do when the humans come hunting for wolves?

The *Sahara's Plight* collection set includes an autographed copy of the book, an 8" collectable plush (through Wild Republic), and an adoption certificate. It can also be purchased through the Nature's Guardian website.

M'vita's Struggle

Having a big family means never wanting for anything. You have protection, loyalty, friendship, and affection. Most of all, you're never alone. But what happens if all of that is taken away?

M'vita was born into a large wild dog family, one of the largest ever seen. But when disaster strikes, she finds herself all alone, the sole survivor in a land of paradise without a single wild dog in sight.

Now, she has to find a way to survive and cope with her loneliness. Squaring off against predators three times her size, she comes to terms with her new role and makes unlikely allies in order to survive. After confiding her fears to an equally lost cheetah, will she finally find what she has been searching for?

About the Author

Alisha M. Kent is a full-time student at Southern New Hampshire University working toward a BA in Creative Writing with a minor in Graphic Design. She is also a full-time writer and illustrator and a full-time mother of four (three of which are special needs). Her passions are reading, writing, drawing, photography, animals, and anything Japanese.

Passionate about animals and the future of the environment, she researches current and past events and works closely with conservation groups to ensure the information is as accurate and up to date as possible.

She currently lives in Texas with her family, her cat, birds, and two rescued turtles.

www.ingramcontent.com/pod-product-compliance
Lightning Source LLC
Chambersburg PA
CBHW062146280526
45788CB00001B/323